With Love,
    Barbara J Moore
        5/2014

ENDORSEMENT FOR *HIDDEN IN THE VALLEY*

"As a fellow disciple and follower of Jesus Christ, the story and the truths Barbara Moore writes about in *Hidden in the Valley* turn my heart evermore toward our Father in heaven. The power of prayer and God's Word are such a force that no one should miss this anointed book. It is my prayer that everyone that reads and shares this story will be blessed by it as I have been."

—Jon Pauling
singer/songwriter and TV and film producer

Hidden

IN THE Valley

BARBARA J. MOORE

EDITED BY CHRISTINA BERRY TARABOCHIA

WESTBOW·
PRESS
A DIVISION OF THOMAS NELSON
& ZONDERVAN

WestBow Press books may be ordered through booksellers or by contacting:

WestBow Press
A Division of Thomas Nelson
1663 Liberty Drive
Bloomington, IN 47403
www.westbowpress.com
1 (866) 928-1240

Because of the dynamic nature of the Internet, any web addresses or links contained in this book may have changed since publication and may no longer be valid. The views expressed in this work are solely those of the author and do not necessarily reflect the views of the publisher, and the publisher hereby disclaims any responsibility for them.

Scripture quotations taken from the Holy Bible, New Living Translation, copyright 1996, 2004. Used by permission of Tyndale House Publishers, Inc., Wheaton, Illinois 60189. All rights reserved.

Any people depicted in stock imagery provided by Thinkstock are models, and such images are being used for illustrative purposes only. Certain stock imagery © Thinkstock.

ISBN: 978-1-4908-1704-0 (sc)
ISBN: 978-1-4908-1705-7 (hc)
ISBN: 978-1-4908-1703-3 (e)

Library of Congress Control Number: 2013921033

Printed in the United States of America.

WestBow Press rev. date: 3/12/2014

CONTENTS

LIST OF ILLUSTRATIONS

ACKNOWLEDGMENTS

My deep appreciation to the following: the Oregon Trail Hotel & Restaurant staff for your kindness to my family, Baker County Taxi Service for your kindness to me, Elkhorn Denture Services for your extreme efforts, Angel Flight for getting Mom and I home, Providence Hospital, Marquis Centennial Rehabilitation Home, and everyone else I have forgotten to mention who cared, helped, and prayed.

To my beautiful McKenna, you were my biggest cheerleader; my beautiful Jordan, for transcribing; my family and friends, for your patience, as you have heard versions of this story countless times; Keith and Kimi Richardson, for your counsel and friendship; Melissa and Scott Leslie, for your love and support; Leila Rae Sommerfield, for your wisdom; Jeff Warila; Ron De Shazer; and everyone who has supported, believed in me, and encouraged me in this endeavor. Thank you!

FOREWORD BY DORIS ANDERSON

Before I got lost, I was discouraged and believed that God didn't love me anymore. It seemed that my prayers weren't being answered, so I thought God didn't have time to help me. I knew many people were praying to Him, and I thought He would get to me when He wasn't so busy helping everyone else. Perhaps someday He would have time to answer my prayers.

While lost in the wilderness, I was alone, tired, cold, hungry, and afraid. My fear was that the evil one was trying to get other people to move away from God and was trying to do the same with me.

Through this experience, I now know how much God loves me because He kept me alive without proper food, kept me safe from wild animals, and sent people to find and rescue me. He answered my cry for help and kept me alive those fourteen days. He led me to a hiding place from the animals and led the rescuers to where I was. They took me to a hospital in Baker County where I got well enough to go back home to recover.

Now I feel like I did before the hunting trip with my husband. I'm pain-free. I'm thankful for a warm bed at night. I'm thankful to God that He did not let me die in the forest. I'm thankful for the people He sent to rescue me. I'm thankful for the people who helped me recover. And I'm not afraid of the dark anymore.

PREFACE

As the daughter of Harold and Doris Anderson, it's my great privilege to tell this story. I'm confident that I am the right person for the job since this is about my family's experience. I suffered along with my father and other family members through the dark days when my mom was missing. I also spent the first seven days at Mom's bedside in Baker City's St. Elizabeth's Hospital after her rescue.

Upon returning to my home while Mom was at Portland's Providence Hospital recovering, I knew there needed to be a book about what happened, and I was compelled to write it. My brother-in-law pointed out that my mom walked through Psalm 23. I was amazed to discover during the writing that each chapter truly correlated with a portion of the well-known passage.

As part of my research, I read Phillip W. Keller's *A Shepherd Looks at Psalm 23*. Keller's knowledge from being a shepherd himself for more than eight years as well as a pastor brought light and new meaning to the words of David, the shepherd boy who wrote the poem, and a greater insight and understanding as to what my mother may have experienced while on the mountain.

For my research, I also traveled to Oregon's Wallowa Mountains in August 2008, a year after my mother's ordeal, and retraced my parents' steps with the help of Sergeant Travis Ash and Oregon State Trooper Chris Hawkins, the officers who found Mom. I also interviewed Chris Galiszewski, the search and rescue coordinator who sequenced the events and shared maps and pictures with me. Many of the key players who took part in this story were gracious with their time, enabling me to tell the story accurately.

This is a journey fueled by emotion, inspiration, and power, and could not go untold because the message is truly transformational. This world can be such a dark place, and it's my desire to light it up one heart at a time. To everyone who has ever worried, been afraid, or needed encouragement, I wrote this for you. And if you have ever questioned your value or significance or wondered whether your life has purpose, I wrote this for you.

To all who like a story with drama, conflict, mystery, and suspense, I sincerely hope you'll enjoy this book as much as I did writing it.

So it's with great honor that I present *Hidden in the Valley*.

Missing person flier

Introduction

LOST

"Hello?" I answered after fumbling for the phone in the dark. "Barb, I just got done talking with the Baker County sheriff. Dad is in the hospital." My sister Cheryl's voice poured from the other end of the phone.

"What? What happened?" I wondered whether I was dreaming, but then I heard Cheryl's voice again.

"Dad and Mom went hunting, and Dad broke his wrist. He's going to be okay, but Mom's not with him."

I rubbed my eyes and looked at the clock. "It's 11:30 at night. Where is she?"

"They don't know. She's still on the mountain. They're looking for her now."

Cheryl's answer shook reality into my sleepy head. "They went hunting without telling us? Is Mom in the car?" I asked.

"They're hoping that's where she is." I heard fear in Cheryl's voice.

"Let's pray that they find her quickly," I said, sensing the jeopardy our mother could be in.

After Cheryl and I got off the phone, I sat in bed, dazed by the shock. How could this be happening? My worry about my parents kept me awake. I wondered whether Cheryl was picturing Mom safe in their Chevy Tahoe like I was. Knowing the fear that gripped our mom, I couldn't imagine her anywhere except in the vehicle behind locked doors.

Throughout the night, I called the hospital numerous times, checking on our dad and getting more information about where Mom was. The sheriff assured me searchers were on their way to where Dad had last seen her on the mountain.

Restless, I called the sheriff's dispatch again to find out whether there was any news. At 4:00 a.m., the dispatcher told me the searchers were bedding down until daylight. They had found the Tahoe, but my mom was not in it. That's the moment fear gripped my heart too. Out in the cold, dark night, my mom was lost in the wilderness.

Doris Anderson is my mother. At seventy-six years old, she made international news in 2007 during her disappearance and extreme rescue from the rugged Wallowa Mountains in northeastern Oregon.

No one could possibly understand what a wonder this is without a glimpse into my mother's life prior to her disappearance. The truth is she needed to be rescued long before the elk hunting trip she took with my father. My mother had weaknesses that made her survival nothing less than phenomenal. Mom was overcome by powerful enemies too strong for her and couldn't escape their grip: fear and worry. They constantly tormented her and robbed her of peace of mind and rest. They were the bad guys who came to get her every night in the darkness.

"Doris!" Dad would yell out. "What are you doing prowling around with that flashlight?"

"Someone's out there. Can't you hear them?" Mom would whisper. "I'm going to check the house and make sure they can't get in."

What could my family do to make my mom feel safe? We couldn't see her invisible villains, yet her agony was visible to us all, and we cried out to the Lord to deliver her from her suffering. It never entered our minds that our loved one would be lost in the wilderness, alone in the dark, surrounded by bears and mountain lions.

I love my mom with all my heart and respect her privacy. I admire her great strength of character and believe she is the kindest, gentlest, and most unselfish woman I have ever known. I don't tell my mom's story without her permission. She has bravely given me freedom to paint a vivid picture revealing her flaws to the world for the purpose of bringing light into somebody else's darkness and hope that freedom exists for those who struggle with emotional and mental bondage.

For as long as I can remember, my mom has struggled with fear. Perhaps, however, *struggled* isn't the correct word, since she never really fought it. Fear has been her companion, even part of her identity. Fear and his brother worry have lived with my mom for who knows how long. Many times she has told me it's better to be cautious and stay safe.

I don't know when these relationships began. Maybe when her father died? She was four years old when she lost him. Who would protect her? She tells a story about when she was seven and living in Mississippi. Mom was walking home from school and a group of girls told her a rabid dog was chasing her. Terrified, she ran all the way home. She later found out they had made it up. I think her enemies found an open door because of her weaknesses and snuck in.

As the years passed and other tragedies occurred, fear and worry took over more in my mom's life. David, my brother and the firstborn son in our family, was diagnosed with cancer and died at age ten. Mom's heart was crushed. Several years later her big brother, Willie, died from a heart attack. She had viewed him as her protector since her father's death.

Next her husband and my father, Harold, had a close encounter with death, just escaping by a thread as his leg was nearly sawed off while logging in Alaska. He almost bled to death. Mom was thousands of miles away in Oregon. I can still see my mom dropping to her knees in horror when she received that call.

His surgeon told her, "He only missed severing the main artery by a hair." Dad spent six months in a body cast, followed by months of therapy and a slow recovery. Mom selflessly took care of him.

Regretfully, my sister, Cheryl, and I were used to add ammunition to fear and worry's attacks on our mother's soul as we carelessly and defiantly stumbled through our adolescence. All the grief of these events propelled her further into the grip of her enemies.

Before the hunting trip with my father, our mother was oppressed, held hostage, and imprisoned in her own body. She was afraid both inside and outside the house. She was afraid of being robbed, not realizing she already had been. Mom had no quality of life. We loved her so much, yet we were unable to alleviate her distress. Who could rescue her from all this?

One night I stayed at Mom's house looking for answers. My family had been praying for revelation about what was causing her trouble. Was she going out of her mind? My brother-in-law wondered whether it was dementia. It seemed to me that I had just laid my head on the pillow when I heard Mom checking doors. I found her up in the middle of the night with the flashlight.

"Someone's outside. Can't you hear them?" she asked me.

"No, Mom, I don't hear anything." But I felt it: there was a strong evil presence that made the hair on my neck and arms stand up.

Following the example of what Jesus did when demons were present, I took authority over them and ordered them to go away. It worked because afterward there was peace in the house, and Mom and I were both able to go back to sleep. That's when the Lord showed me Mom was not hearing things or crazy: spirits were tormenting her, and there are no pills to make that go away.

My dad had been planning his annual elk hunting trip and thought it would be great to get Mom out of the house and into the beautiful surroundings of the mountains. He was about at his wit's end with my mom's fears. Dad loved the mountains, especially the Wallowas. To him it was a piece of heaven.

In their younger years, my parents had enjoyed camping, hunting, and fishing together. So Dad invited Mom to go elk hunting with him. This was the start of their misadventure and the beginning of my mom's journey through Psalm 23.

THE SHEPHERD

by Kristina Smith

FOLLOW YOUR HEART

"The Lord is my Shepherd,
I have everything I need."
—Psalm 23:1–2

In early August 2007, my family unknowingly was headed for a storm. Summer had swept by, with my sister and I busy with kids and work, yet somehow we had made time to visit with each other.

Cheryl and her husband, Harvey, were always on the run with their six children: Kristina, Kindel, Rene, Shania, Shianne, and Joshua, plus baby Caleb was on his way. I had two beautiful girls of my own, Jordan Ashley and McKenna. I ran a vacation rental cleaning business and was glad Cheryl was working with me through the busy summer break.

Mom and Dad were on our hearts during this time. Cheryl hadn't talked to them for a week or so, and I hadn't spoken to them since my birthday on July 19. We knew they were going elk hunting sometime during the month, and we were worried about the trip.

The Wallowa-Whitman National Forest is in the northeast corner of Oregon, 365 miles away from our homes. We knew they might leave without telling us because Dad was impulsive. When he wanted to do something, there was no holding him back.

My dad and Harvey had gone bow hunting for elk several years in a row in the Wallowas. They loved to hunt there because of the beautiful high country. "The snowcapped peaks of these mountains are so captivating, they simply draw you in," Harvey once explained.

**Picture of the snowcapped mountain peaks
of Oregon's Eagle Cap Wilderness**

Two Colors Campground

Dad and his Quad

In 2006, Dad and Harvey hunted by Two Colors Lake. Harvey was riding Dad's quad ATV with Dad on the back when they hit a rut in the road; the vehicle rolled over. Dad broke some ribs and came within inches of a tree branch piercing his temple.

Harvey lifted the six-hundred-pound vehicle off its side to get them out of there. He still doesn't know where the strength came from.

Harvey got scared in the remote, isolated territory. Baker City was the nearest town with medical help and was more than an hour-and-a-half drive.

Because of the dense canopy of ponderosa pine, fir, spruce, and hemlock trees, cell phones did not pick up signals in the mountain range. Harvey realized the trouble they could have been in. He imagined our mom asking him why he had killed her husband. Though they lived to tell the tale, it was the last hunting trip Harvey would take with my dad.

I had a gut-wrenching feeling I couldn't shake. What would Mom do if Dad got hurt? Because of her fear, I felt she wouldn't be able to help him much. Harvey, Cheryl, and I followed our hearts' leading and we prayed. We asked the Lord to stop them from going on this trip if they were not supposed to go. We were compelled to pray about the trip on three separate occasions during those first weeks of August.

In the meantime, Harvey asked Dad not to take Mom on the hunting trip. Although Cheryl and I were concerned as well, neither of us called Mom or Dad. We chose to put our trust in the Lord and left the details in His hands. Our practice of trusting God is what kept us sane.

My favorite Bible verse, Proverbs 3:5, says, "Trust in the Lord with all your heart, in all your ways acknowledge Him, and He will direct your path." From the depth of our hearts, we truly believed the Lord loved Mom and Dad more than we could love them. His love is perfect. We also trusted that the Lord knew our mom and dad's needs before we asked for His intervention.

To explain, the Lord, known also as the Good Shepherd, always goes out ahead of His sheep. A shepherd is aware of all the dangers of the wild. We understand that we're limited, but He is I Am. God identified Himself to Abraham by this name. I Am, in essence, means sufficient for all things at all times.

On Saturday night, August 25, our earlier concerns and discernment about this trip became reality. Dad did get hurt, and he had left Mom to go for help. Now our mom was somewhere up on a mountain in the wilderness, and she needed to be rescued.

BY PEACEFUL STREAMS
by Kristina Smith

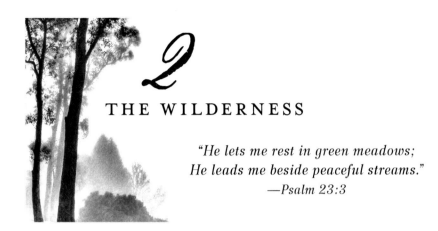

THE WILDERNESS

"He lets me rest in green meadows;
He leads me beside peaceful streams."
—*Psalm 23:3*

St. Elizabeth's Hospital in eastern Oregon released Dad, although he would need surgery on his wrist within seven days. Baker County Sheriff Mitch Southwick and Undersheriff Warren Thompson were in charge of the investigation concerning Mom's disappearance. The two officers questioned Dad. His help in putting the pieces together was crucial.

The officers pressed Dad for answers because of the urgency of finding Mom in the treacherous territory before nightfall. They needed to understand what happened and pinpoint the exact location where he had last seen her. Dad was worried, afraid, exhausted, traumatized, and even borderline incoherent. He tried to recall the details of what had happened and wanted to help them find Mom, but he could barely hold himself together.

The Wallowa Mountains had been the backdrop for many people's adventures. Unfortunately, my mom and dad's adventure turned into a misadventure right out of the gate. Mom and Dad had headed for Two Colors Campground. From there, they planned to go another five miles up to Two Colors Lake. Dad loved the alpine meadows laced with Indian paintbrush, larkspur, bluebells, and shooting stars. Up on high ground at seven thousand feet, the stars were magnificent and seemed close enough that you could reach up and touch them. Most importantly, my dad hoped to see Rocky Mountain elk.

An alpine meadow

Dad had prepared for the trip for months. To say he was excited would be an understatement. Bow-hunting season ran from the last week of August through the last week of September. My dad was like a kid when it came to hunting. He could hardly wait to go and wouldn't think or talk about anything else until he reached his destination. It never really seemed to matter whether he got an elk.

Mom and Dad arrived in Union, Oregon, on Thursday morning, August 23, and stopped at a restaurant for breakfast. The next stop would be the Wallowa-Whitman National Forest where they would scope out their campsite. They parked their Chevy Tahoe off the 025 forest service road at Two Colors Campground and quickly unloaded Dad's quad. Ready for an adventure, they took off on the ATV, headed for high country.

Dad at Two Colors Lake Campground with his
SUV, utility trailer, ATV and ATV trailer

Dad (in camouflage) on high ground from
his 2006 hunting trip with Harvey

Once through the gate and out of the campground, my parents' adventure came to an abrupt halt: they couldn't get up to the meadows because the forest service had closed the road to vehicles. My dad's anticipation that had built while waiting for bow season to arrive plummeted. To have gotten so close and to find the road blocked, Dad was faced with an obstacle he could not cross over without breaking the law.

Road blocked by forest service

Dad felt disappointed that he had driven so far only to find the road blocked. His favorite hunting ground was just on the other side, out of his reach. His first response was to turn around and go home. Mom was fine with that because she had been nearly scared to death by a black bear they saw in the campground.

Discouraged, they made it back to the Tahoe and prepared to load the ATV. Dad got on the vehicle first and rode it up the ramp and into the larger utility trailer. Then he pushed the smaller ATV trailer up the ramp to be loaded, standing it on end to make it fit, but the trailer fell backward, dropping on his left wrist, breaking it, and then knocking him sideways off the tailgate. Dad got caught by his boot and was trapped between the tailgate and ATV trailer. He hung upside down from the ramp until Mom could release him.

Once free, my then seventy-four-year-old father dropped to the ground and laid there in the dirt for some time in pain. Besides his wrist, he had also hurt his hip and leg. Further complicating matters, he was already at a deficit because of prior injuries. The previously mentioned logging accident he had in 1976 left him missing an inch of bone from his right leg, decreasing his mobility and throwing his right side off balance. His left side was equally challenged after shattering his hip in a fall in 2004; steel, wires, and screws held his hip together. So the combination of my dad's age, his past injuries, and the twisting and contorting he went through plus a broken wrist and possible head trauma equaled nothing but trouble.

Our worst fears about my father being hurt had come true. My mother had to come through and help him. After she released him from the tailgate, she had to get him back up on his feet because he couldn't stand on his own. Then she had to help him reload the trailer that had fallen on him. She also had to help him lift and close the heavy gate ramp to secure the large utility trailer, difficult even for two younger people with the use of both arms. Once loaded up and in the Tahoe, they headed out.

Dad, disoriented and in shock from the pain, turned the wrong way. Instead of making a right off the 025 road and going back to 7700, the main road out, he mistakenly turned left onto forest service road 7750 and headed deeper into the wilderness. He maneuvered the Tahoe and fully loaded trailer down an old, rough, rocky, remote one-lane road. He had to drive with only one hand because of the pain of his broken wrist. Mom didn't drive. She used to, but that was another area of her life lost to fear.

The long winding stretch of the unimproved 7750 road was uphill, rutted, and rocky, making it difficult to drive on. Canyons with steep drop-offs into creek bottoms hundreds of feet below lined the way. The only place wide enough to turn around with the trailer came at Bennet Creek. Why he did not turn around there, we don't know. Perhaps because he was headed downhill, he thought eventually they would get out.

11

7750, the wrong road

They winded off on the 422 spur road, ending up at an old mine known as O'Brien Creek. The road worsened and abruptly dropped several feet where part had washed out. My dad couldn't maneuver the vehicle with the fully loaded utility trailer because the road was too narrow.

Knowing he could go no farther, my dad spent half an hour struggling to turn around in the narrow place. Slowly, he made progress until the rear trailer wheel slipped off the edge of the road and the vehicle high centered, which means the tongue, or tow hitch of the vehicle, dug into the ground like a jack, lifting the tires off the ground so they couldn't get traction to move. Stuck, my parents spent the night in the truck.

Around 8:00 a.m., they discussed what they needed to do. I can only imagine the conversation that must have taken place as concern shifted to fear and worry. The reality of all the mistakes they had made set in. Dad wanted to walk for help. Mom wanted to stay at the truck, sure Harvey and Cheryl would come for them. Dad didn't think anyone would come because no one knew where they were. Only my mom's best friend, Mary, knew when they had left

7750, with steep drop-offs into canyons

I can only guess what my parents' mental and physical state was at that point. To begin with, they had plenty of food and water in the vehicle, enough to last several weeks. They had solar blankets and lots of other supplies. For this reason, I don't understand why they set out carrying nothing with them other than Mom's purse. Dad had expensive camping equipment. He had a backpack. Maybe he

13

The old O'Brien Creek mine

The old O'Brien Creek mine

didn't want to mess with putting it on because of his painful wrist, but why didn't they put it on Mom? I can't imagine my parents in such an isolated place heading out into the wilderness with nothing other than my mom's purse.

At 5,200-feet elevation, O'Brien Creek's temperature can fluctuate by forty degrees and ranged in the twenties to thirties at night, although during the day the average was in the eighties.

The end of the road

The road my parents were stranded on

On the first morning after my parents became stranded, they started off on foot to find help. The way out of the wilderness was a steep, uneven climb up a road full of holes. This steep incline was difficult for my dad with his injuries and hard for my mom, too. They walked for 1.6 miles before they reached level ground. Exhausted, they stopped at the fork of forest service roads 250 and 7750, laid down in a green meadow under the shade of a tree, and took a nap.

The green meadow at 250 and 7750 where my parents napped

When they woke up, they continued walking along forest service road 7750. They made it another 2.25 miles in the hot sun without water when Mom heard something. As they rounded the corner to the next meadow, Mom heard the sound of water from a stream. The meadow was the entrance to the Bennet Creek Drainage.

"Harold, I'm thirsty. Will you go down to that stream with me?" she asked.

"I'm worried that I won't make it back up if I go down there," he told her. "We have to keep going to find help."

"I don't want to go any farther. Can we go back to the truck?"

"I'll give you my keys and you can go back. I have to keep going and find help." He pulled his keys out of his pocket. "Put these in your purse."

Mom opened her purse and took out the bag that she always carried with her containing her most precious items, such as jewelry pieces. She worried that someone might steal them and always kept her treasures near her. Looking Dad in the eyes, she handed over her treasures: "Keep these, okay?"

After telling each other to be careful, they parted ways. Dad says he left Mom in good spirits. Since she did not freak out, as we would have expected, perhaps she was trying to be brave for him. Later we learned she had told her friend Mary she didn't think she was going to come home. It seems as though Cheryl, Harvey, and I were not the only ones with discernment.

It was still daylight as Mom walked back toward the truck and out of Dad's sight. He then continued down the 7750 road to find help. He only made it another 1.5 miles before he collapsed next to a log.

The log where the Buckmaster party found Dad

A hunting party led by a man named Terry Buckmaster found Dad at 3:00 p.m. Saturday. I assume Dad was unconscious for some time since thirty-one hours had passed since he and Mom had started walking out from the vehicle until the hunting party reached him. He had traveled only 5.6 miles by foot. Dad had spent the night out in the cold and recalled sitting on a log, unable to stop shivering. Dad managed to tell Buckmaster about the stranded Tahoe and Mom, though he did not seem totally coherent.

The hunting party took him back to the stranded vehicle to get Mom, but she was not there. The trailer was unhooked from the Tahoe, the ATV was unloaded, and supplies were scattered across the rocky ground. Dad remembered he had attempted to ride his quad out, but it wouldn't start. Buckmaster and his party put everything away, hooked up the trailer, and told Dad to get in the truck and start it so they could tow him out.

"I gave my keys to my wife," he said. Buckmaster then realized Dad was not thinking straight. They spent all that time working toward getting the vehicle out, and then he remembered he didn't have the keys? Dad had counted on Mom being at the truck.

"Where's my wife?" Dad asked. Fear and worry about her safety had caused his face to go white and his stomach to sicken.

The hunting party saw Dad's distress and thought they better get my dad into town, get medical help for him, and contact the sheriff's office for help.

At 7:45 p.m., Dad arrived at St Elizabeth's. The Baker County Sheriff's Department was contacted, and Dad and the Buckmaster party reported that Mom was missing in the Eagle Creek area. Deputy John Hoopes took the report. Dispatch contacted Chris Galiszewski, the search and rescue coordinator for the sheriff's department. Galiszewski organized the search mission and sent an eight-person team of search and rescue volunteers to meet with the sheriff at his office.

The search team went to the Buckmaster campsite for assistance locating the log where Dad was found and the spot where the stranded vehicle was.

The search team planned a hasty search of the area. The goal was to cover the roads, get to the vehicle, and preserve the scene. They split up so they could cover both ends of the 5.6 miles of road from the log to the vehicle. They worked until 4:00 a.m. and then bedded down. At that point, my family and all the searchers trying to find my mom were in the dark waiting for daybreak.

The search resumed at daylight on Sunday, August 26. It was the third day since Mom and Dad had separated, and a full-scale investigation was under way. While back at home, my family spent the early morning hours gathering details about what had happened and deciding what to do. I stayed home for our kids, and my sister and Harvey headed for the Baker County Sheriff's Department to help Dad. Dispatch told my family that more than forty searchers were doing a grid search from the Tahoe to the area where my mom and dad had parted. They promised to keep us informed.

The search and rescue team had a list of questions for the sheriff to ask Dad Sunday morning. Did Mom have a phone? Did she have a plan, a weapon with ammo and, if so, did she know how to use it? Was she taking any medications? Did she have food or water? Was she mentally stable?

Unfortunately, the answer to all these questions was no, except Dad didn't know Mom's mental condition. She only had her purse with her and was lightly dressed.

Sheriff Southwick thought Dad seemed confused, which made sense since Dad hadn't slept for three nights and was injured. Besides the exhaustion, he was mentally and emotionally traumatized because his wife was missing.

Dad returned to the wilderness that morning with the sheriff to point out the places he and Mom had been. The questioning was extremely tiresome, as Dad felt he was answering the same questions repeatedly.

Harvey and Cheryl were on the road, estimating a three-and-a-half-hour drive to Baker City. In the meantime, Galiszewski lined up more people from Baker County search and rescue. At 7:30 a.m., he brought in ten additional search and rescue team members to cover the main roads and close down the area. They needed to restrict access to the territory Mom could have covered on foot and preserve clues. They searched for footprints or any other sign that might lead them to her.

Two scent-detecting dogs and handlers also were brought in from the Wallowa County K-9 unit in the hopes they could pick up Mom's trail. In addition to ground search, an airplane searched from 9:00 a.m. to noon that Sunday.

Adding to Harvey and Cheryl's tension, a tire blew out on their vehicle while they were traveling sixty miles per hour on the freeway on the way to Baker City. Their fear was compounded because a semi truck was in the lane next to them. "It was a miracle no one was hurt. Thank God he sends his angels to protect us," Harvey later said.

It was difficult to even get back on the road because most tire stores weren't open on Sunday. When Harvey and Cheryl finally arrived at the Baker County Sheriff's Department, Dad was being interrogated for the third time.

Dad, growing impatient, continued to answer the sheriff with "I already told you that."

The sheriff's concern was reflected in his response: "Harold, we are just trying to find her."

Harvey and Cheryl wanted to help look for Mom, but the authorities would not let them, afraid Harvey and Cheryl also would end up lost.

By the time Cheryl and Harvey saw Dad, he looked like he hadn't slept for days and probably felt like it too. They both saw the anxiety on Dad's face written in his deep frown lines and squinted glare.

"Good, you're here. Let's go home." Dad rattled out the words and rushed for the exit. He couldn't get out of the sheriff's department fast enough.

Cheryl's focus at the time was to get Dad somewhere so he could rest. The Oregon Trail Motel & Restaurant employees warmly welcomed my family members and offered hospitality, kindness, and empathy. In the small town of Baker City, news traveled fast. Most of the locals had heard about the elderly woman missing near the Eagle Cap Wilderness. Pam Linderman, part owner of the Oregon Trail, gave my family a nice room and insisted on taking care of meals while they were in Baker City.

The search was intensive that Sunday and wrapped up around 9:00 p.m.

Back at their motel room that evening, Dad, Cheryl, and Harvey opened the door for fresh air. No more than a few minutes after darkness descended, they were forced to shut the door to keep out the cold. At that moment, they realized the danger Mom was in from exposure to the cold temperature. It was only thirty degrees in Baker City, and Mom was another three thousand feet higher with no protection.

Overwhelmed by helplessness and flooded with waves of guilt and despair, especially during the black of night, they each experienced heartbreak for Mom's suffering. Harvey has visions and dreamed of Mom in a ravine that night.

At 5:15 a.m. on Monday, August 27, day four of the ordeal, Galiszewski continued the search with the plan he had prepared for the day. Twenty search and rescue volunteers, divided with fourteen US Forest Service crews, would team up: one search and rescue member with two to three forest service firefighters and supervisors.

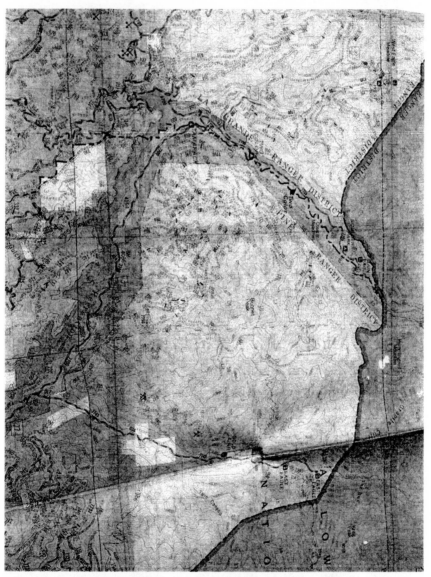

Forest Service map of Eagle Creek area

Considering Harvey's dream, both Harvey and I asked dispatch if the teams were searching the ravines. They told us they were. In fact, the goal for that day was to cover O'Brien Creek and Bennet Creek Drainage, two of the main ravines with water. Both of these areas would be grid searched, meaning five to twenty people would stand in a line and walkthrough the area, maintaining the straight line, while leaving no stone unturned. They would check all the houses and cabins along Eagle Creek Road and East Eagle Creek as well.

An Oregon National Guard OH-58 Kiowa helicopter with thermal imaging equipment on board was on the scene Monday too. Unfortunately, the thermal imaging was not effective because of the density of the trees.

Dad was called into the sheriff's office at least twice a day for twenty-minute sessions of intense interrogation. He didn't like this and took offense, feeling as if his words were meaningless because the authorities asked the same questions again and again.

At 6:00 a.m. on Tuesday, August 28, the search group gathered, consisting of three off-duty deputies, Marine Patrol deputies, six search and rescue members, crews from LaGrande Forest Service, a four-person engine crew from Baker City, and crews from Halfway, Oregon. The day's mission was to cover from the 250 forest service road all the way back up the 7750 road. The entire distance from my parents' napping point to the original campsite would be searched

During all this, Cheryl and Harvey were not permitted to go far from the sheriff's department with Dad, who was continually placed in the hot seat and grilled by Undersheriff Thompson. Most searches did not extend beyond two 24-hour periods, which had been exceeded in my mom's case with no results.

The searchers couldn't find a trace of Mom. They couldn't place her outside the vehicle. It was as if she had never been there at all. Where was she? Had she really been here? Did my dad leave her at home? Why did they leave the vehicle without supplies? The sheriff was doing his job in investigating every angle, but Dad felt the sheriff thought Dad had murdered Mom.

At 6:00 a.m. on Wednesday, August 29, the sixth day, the searching carried on as three K-9 air scent dogs from Wallowa County and a Yamhill County team sniffed out the valleys. The sheriff and undersheriff were joined by four fire service volunteers plus two more men from another fire crew.

The phrase of the day was "probability of detection," addressing how well the searchers covered the terrain. They also tacked missing person fliers to fence posts and trees where they were searching and also around Baker City and Union. Droves of bow hunters were in the area, so one of them might stumble across my mom. Sheriff Southwick told my sister that it didn't look good and cautioned her to expect the worst.

Dad was interrogated once more and no longer could keep his cool. Emotionally charged by frustration and anger, he blurted out hotly, "You think I'm lying, don't you? You think I murdered my wife! Do you have any reason to keep me here?"

The sheriff was also frustrated and continued to repeat, "Harold, we are just trying to find her. You were the last one to see her, and you're our only link."

The sheriff wanted Dad to stay, but Cheryl and Harvey convinced the authorities to let Dad go home. They were not going to get any more information out of him.

It took fifteen hours to tow the Tahoe from where it had been stuck. Dad signed papers releasing it to the sheriff's department. The authorities would now examine it thoroughly to see if they could find any kind of evidence.

My family's experience in Baker City, Oregon, left them with a bittersweet taste in their mouths. On one hand, it was a slice of heaven meeting and receiving help from some of the nicest people in the world. Harvey commented it was the best place to be if you were in trouble. On the other hand, they had never experienced such dark, seemingly never-ending days. Cheryl was anxious to get Dad out of there and get him home.

As they left Baker City, Dad said to Cheryl, "I left the best piece of myself on that mountain."

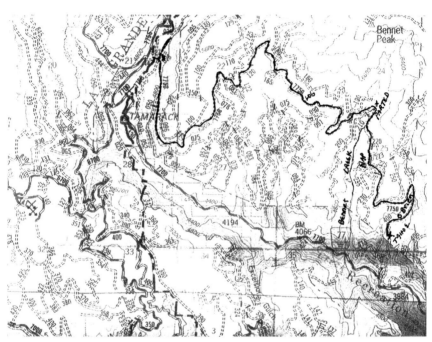

**Map showing how far Mom and Dad
traveled down the wrong road**

WALKING THROUGH THE VALLEY
by Kristina Smith

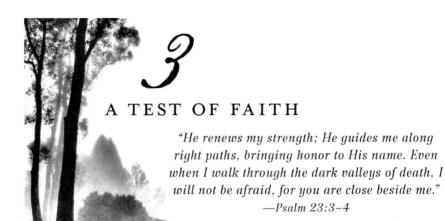

3

A TEST OF FAITH

*"He renews my strength; He guides me along
right paths, bringing honor to His name. Even
when I walk through the dark valleys of death, I
will not be afraid, for you are close beside me."*
—Psalm 23:3–4

The morning after I learned my mother was missing in the wilderness, I came undone. I was supposed to teach a Sunday school class at church, but every bit of strength and energy I had was directed at praying for Mom. Cheryl, Harvey, and I had joined our faith with our church, family, and friends, and it seemed as if we prayed without ceasing from the moment we got the news Mom was lost. Knowing there was strength in numbers, I also asked my neighbors and dear friends Tom and Taeler Butel to pray in agreement with me after Cheryl and Harvey left for Baker City.

Walking through this dark valley was a chance to experience the real meaning of faith. Another friend of the family, Pastor Rod Smith, once challenged us when he said, "It is one thing to say what you believe. What have you proved out? 'Faith is the confidence that what we hope for will actually happen; it gives us assurance about things we cannot see.'"[1]

During difficult times when my faith and patience are being challenged, I look to the Bible for encouragement and remind myself:

To follow the example of those who are going to inherit God's promises because of their faith and endurance. For example, there was God's promise to Abraham. Since there was no one greater to swear by, God took an oath in his own name, saying: "I will certainly bless you, and I will multiply your descendants beyond number." Then Abraham waited patiently, and he received what

---

1   Hebrews 11:1

God had promised. Now when people take an oath, they call on someone greater than themselves to hold them to it. And without any question that oath is binding. God also bound himself with an oath, so that those who received the promise could be perfectly sure that He would never change His mind. So God has given both his promise and his oath. These two things are unchangeable because it is impossible for God to lie. Therefore, we who have fled to him for refuge can have great confidence as we hold to the hope that lies before us. This hope is a strong and trustworthy anchor for our souls.[2]

This is one of my favorite descriptions in the Bible of how faith holds us steady in times of trial.

We are also told that "the angels are ministering spirits sent forth to serve those who are heirs of salvation."[3] Believers have the legal right to be saved from everything—nothing missing, nothing broken. The Bible is God's will and testament to His children. All that belongs to God the Father transferred through His Son's death to all who believe and take hold of the benefits or promises.

My mom was an heir of salvation, so Tom, Taeler, and I sent the angels to surround her, protect her, and keep the wild animals away from her. We knew Mom was afraid, and we asked the Holy Spirit to be her peace and comfort her. Then we asked God to send the rescuers to find her. We asked God to restore her. We asked for a great testimony to come out of this so that the world would know that God had saved her.

We declared she would live and not die and that His glory would be revealed to the earth. Finally, we released our faith into the heavens. That was our prayer. Now we would have to walk it out and trust God.

Later that afternoon, I stripped the laundry from the vacation rental cottages at Mt. Hood Village Resort and stayed busy to pass the time. As I was driving through the resort, I heard the Lord say, "Your mom is with Me." Thinking she had left the earth, I cried because I was overwhelmed by grief, believing I had lost her.

---

2   Hebrews 6:12–19
3   Hebrews 1:14

Just then Cheryl called me from a cell phone. "Are you hearing anything?" she asked.

"Yes, I'm hearing Mom is with the Lord."

"Really? Harvey and I are hearing that too."

Cheryl didn't think Mom was alive because of the conversation she had with God on the way to Baker City. She was crying and begged Him, "Please let them find Mom." Every time she asked that of the Lord, she heard the same reply: "She's with Me."

Cheryl didn't know how to interpret this. Perhaps Mom had fallen and gotten hurt. Although her first thought was that Mom was dead, she also heard the Lord say, "I hid her like I hid Moses."

Curious, Cheryl and I looked up the death of Moses in Deuteronomy 34:1–6, the account of Moses going up the mountain, climbing a peak, and the Lord showing him the whole land. Moses was allowed to see the land the Lord had promised to Abraham, Isaac, and Jacob, but he was not allowed to enter it because of his disobedience: "So Moses the servant of the Lord, died there in the land of Moab, just as the Lord had said. The Lord buried him in a valley near Beth-Peor in Moab, but to this day no one knows the exact place. The bones of Moses were never found."

Cheryl wondered if God had taken Mom to heaven. Maybe she was hidden and no one would find her body because God was being gracious and merciful to us, sparing us the sight of her dead body.

I didn't know if Mom had died. Instead, I wondered if maybe the Lord took her up to heaven like He did Elijah and Enoch.[4] These two men didn't die. Maybe, like Mr. Scott in *Star Trek*, He had beamed her up because the fear she had was too much for her. Maybe He had rescued her. As strange as all this sounds, the possibility of this supernatural ending brought peace and comfort to my family.

Cheryl and Harvey were exhausted when they brought Dad home late Wednesday evening. Dad was distressed and had talked nonstop the whole way home. My sister and I decided to stay with him, thinking it would be good for him to have his children and grandchildren around. Cheryl and I needed to take care of our dad. We needed to be together to get through this dark time. We felt as though we had been sucked up in a whirlwind.

---

4   2 Kings 2:1–8

Uncle Bill, Dad's brother, had called the media because he thought that more people knowing Mom was lost would increase her chances of being found because more people would be looking for her. I understood his reasoning, but I couldn't let him give our personal phone numbers to the media. I didn't have any new information to add, and I was being protective of Dad because he really couldn't handle any more questions. Besides, my phone rang constantly, and I already had more calls than I could handle. Our family, friends, and everyone else who had heard the news and knew us wanted to know what was going on.

Cheryl stayed with Dad during the day while Harvey and I went to work. It was extremely difficult to focus on our jobs because of all the emotions and distractions we were experiencing. In addition, it was time for our children's schools to start again. Cheryl, Harvey, and I were trying to get our kids ready for school with the extra challenge of planning and coordinating the driving time to and from Dad's house, work, and school.

It was cramped with four adults and four kids living in Dad's three-bedroom home. It was as though we were all crammed into one little boat trying to navigate our way through this dark storm. We were thrashed by the waves of emotions and tossed back and forth trying to keep commitments, but Jesus was in our boat. I had peace in my soul, but my head didn't know whether I was coming or going. It was hard times, and although we were battered, we were determined to make the best of it. Only our faith kept us anchored.

With each new day, encouragement and hope from the sheriff about finding Mom decreased. The search went on, although the number of searchers had been significantly cut back.

Day seven, Thursday, August 30, the sheriff and undersheriff went out with a K-9 team from Yamhill. The dog handlers wanted to work the dogs during different times of the day. Starting them in the early morning (3:00 a.m.) meant there was less likelihood of other people being out. Also, the morning dew caused scent to intensify or linger, making it easier for dogs to pick up. These dogs specialized in air scent. They were trained to pick up a person's scent and go right to him or her.

A handful of volunteers were left wrapping up the search, as this would be the last official day. They had already set a new benchmark for the longest search in Oregon. Resources, volunteers, and ideas were running out.

Most of the search crew had been volunteers who had taken time off from their jobs. Ranchers left their hay in the fields and came to help too. This could not go on indefinitely. They all felt bad that they had not found Mom, but they didn't know what more could be done. Sheriff Southwick said there was a slight possibility she could have plunged into the steep, brushy Bennet Creek Drainage.

Over Labor Day weekend (August 31 through September 3), search and rescue team members and leaders unofficially searched for Mom. Because they didn't want to give up, they trudged through the thick underbrush calling her name, hunting for her down in the canyons.

While on a camping trip, Sheriff Southwick and his wife, Paula, spent time searching for Mom and ran into Rod Wickham, a search and rescue leader, and his wife, Carmen, trying to find her too. Galiszewski was out on Labor Day looking for her as well. These people personified dedication. Whether official or unofficial, these people were heroes to my family.

It was so hard to be in Mom's house, seeing her pictures and being around her things but missing her presence. Dad, Cheryl, Harvey, and I felt as though the shadow of death over the house would swallow us up. I feared the guilt for leaving Mom out there would consume my dad. She had taken care of him for fifty-five years. How could he survive without her? I loved my dad and didn't want to lose him, but I asked the Lord to mercifully take him in his sleep if it was too painful for him to go on. I didn't want him to suffer for the rest of his life.

One night the darkness overwhelmed me. I cried because I was sad for me, sad I wouldn't be able to tell Mom the things a daughter shares with her mom. McKenna had just learned to ride her bike and tie her shoes—big milestones to a grandma. I couldn't get over the idea of not being able to talk to my mom again.

The darkness felt unbearable, and I needed some light. So I decided to embrace Jesus, the Light of the World, and told Him, "Lord, all I can do is praise You because Mom is free. I will rejoice because she is with You and free from her torment."

The odds were against finding Mom because of her age, the nighttime temperatures, wild animals, and treacherous terrain.

There had also been several storms to add to the misery. The Eagle Cap Wilderness, including Wallowa-Whitman National Forest, encompassed 361,446 acres, or 565 square miles, making Eagle Cap Oregon's largest wilderness area. Finding my mom really was like searching for a needle in a haystack.

Mom was hidden in the valley, and our hearts were prepared for her not to be found. The only thing we knew for sure was that she was with the Lord. God gave us Psalm 18 through my friend Susan, which brought great comfort and peace to my family because we were desperately reaching for hope, especially Dad. We didn't know yet the full impact of these words and what God would do on my mom's behalf.

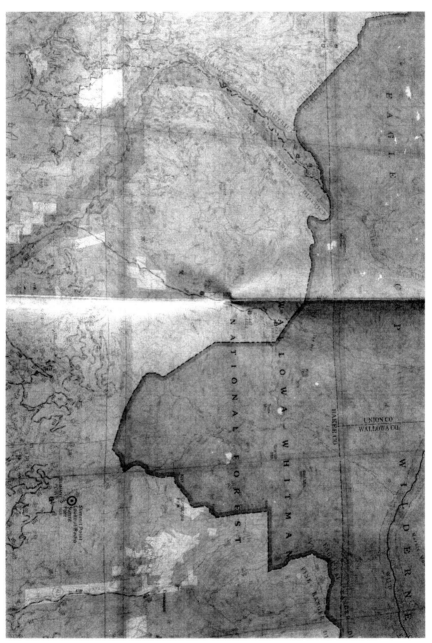

(USFS map of Wallowa-Whitman National Forest)

Officer Travis Ash (His rod) and Chris Hawkins (His staff)

4

AGAINST THE ODDS

"Your rod and staff protect and comfort me."
—*Psalm 23:4*

The sheriff's department had given up hope of finding Mom alive. As for the family, we all were asking ourselves how much longer this could go on. The odds of Mom surviving so many days in the woods seemed nearly impossible. We were suffering.

Since Mom's body had not been found, we had time to plan for a memorial service. We were thinking about our grieving friends and relatives, too, and aware that we all needed some form of closure. However, we had problems picking a date for the service. School was about to start; September 13 was Dad's birthday; September 15 was Cheryl and Harvey's anniversary; September 26 was Shania and Joshua's birthdays. I finally called our pastor and asked if he could make the decision for us.

The sheriff's department wanted closure too. Detective Travis Ash was brought on to the case to start putting pieces together, such as whether my mother had ever been on the mountain or ever returned to the Tahoe. The authorities were not convinced that she had been on the mountain because they didn't find any sign of her.

The truth is, when Detective Ash talked to the trackers, they could not put her outside the vehicle at all. They couldn't find a foot track or anything. The sheriff asked Travis to get Mom's dental records, and he had already contacted Mt. Hood Dental requesting them. He asked the sheriff to let him call Dad, since Detective Ash had never really talked to my father.

Detective Ash called Dad on Wednesday, September 5. He

pressed my father hard, strategically phrasing his questions to get particular answers. Dad, exhausted and volatile from the nightmare he was living through, quickly grew angry. He was outraged that the authorities had the audacity to accuse him again. More than anyone, he suffered because he had left Mom out there alone in the woods. Thoughts of bugs and animals devouring her body tormented him.

After speaking with Dad, Detective Ash knew it wasn't right to give up the search for my mother. He told Dad he was going back to find her. He became convinced Mom was out there somewhere. Although more than one thousand man-hours had been spent combing the area numerous times, the detective had a theory he was compelled to check out. The main thing that convinced the detective that Dad was telling the truth was that his distances of the ground he and Mom had covered were right on track with the detective's own estimations.

After questioning my father, Travis went home and peered over the fence of his neighbor and friend, Oregon State Trooper Chris Hawkins, who was not yet involved in the case. The detective was anxious to discuss his theory regarding where he believed Mom's body could be found.

Spotting his friend, Travis called out, "Hey, Chris! You know that Anderson case the sheriff's been on?"

"Yeah, I know a little about the missing woman. What's up?"

"I just talked to her husband, Harold. Chris, in my gut, I know she's up there somewhere." Travis filled in his friend on the rest of the details then asked, "What do you think? Do you want to go check it out and find her with me?"

"No doubt. Let's go."

"Okay, we're going to find her. Let's meet at my office in the morning." Travis was confident.

After his conversation with Trooper Hawkins, Travis called the undersheriff and said, "You know, I'm going back up to the mountain tomorrow. I want to take a crack at finding Doris."

"Have at it," the undersheriff told him.

Travis, after talking with my father, realized the pain and shock Dad must have been in after breaking his wrist, hitting his head, and hanging upside down from the trailer for at least ten minutes. He also realized how Dad, after the trauma, must have been disoriented and made the wrong turn from the 025 forest service road onto the 7750 road.

Chris, despite not being involved in the case at that point, came to the same conclusion after the scenario was laid out for him. Both he and Travis believed Mom, like an animal, would have gone downhill in a draw that contained water because a weak animal heads for water. Chris knew this because he grew up hunting in the wilderness with his dad. His love of the outdoors led to working in the fish and wildlife division. Chris had great investigative and tracking skills.

On the morning of Thursday, September 6, as Travis prepared to leave home, his wife told him that he would find Doris.

At 8:00 a.m., Travis and Chris headed out, confident they would find my mother. They went to Travis' office first and discussed their plan with Undersheriff Thompson.

"Go make something happen!" he told the men.

Hawkins said, "Okay, we will."

Travis nodded in agreement. He and Chris both had the attitude that they were going to find my mother, Doris Anderson.

"I believe you two will," Thompson said with a grin. "So I'll be up on the Eagle Road around 12:00 p.m."

Because signals from the officers' satellite radios would not reach the Baker County Sheriff's Department from the remote area they would be searching, Undersheriff Thompson told the men he would be standing by on the Eagle Road so they could radio him directly when they found her body. The two friends headed for the south side of the Eagle Cap Wilderness, sure they would find my mother.

Much of the area was inaccessible except by ATV or on foot. Knowing Mom had been thirsty and headed toward water, the men were going to search the creeks and look for scavenger birds that would be attracted to a body.

They started on the 7750 forest service road around noon and were preparing to unload their four-wheel ATVs when they heard ravens crying and knew it was a sign that Mom's body was nearby. While back at home in Sandy, Oregon, at noon on September 6, Dad saw a white dove sitting on a wire as he got the mail. In the Bible, a white dove represented the Spirit of God as well as peace and hope. Dad told my sister it was a sign that somehow everything would be all right.

Meanwhile, Travis and Chris left one of their ATVs at O'Brien Creek where my parents' Tahoe had been stranded. Next they doubled up on the other vehicle and rode uphill to the meadow where they still heard ravens crying from below the ridge at the bottom of Bennet Creek Drainage.

The two moved quickly down the steep slope trying to find the birds but began sliding and falling, grasping at bushes to stay upright. They went halfway down the hillside, sat, watched, listened, and waited, but never saw or heard the ravens again.

With the birds gone and nothing else to go on, they could have given up, presuming there was nothing in the Bennet Creek area. Only their determination not to miss my mother and the belief they would find her drove them on.

After climbing back up the slope, they dropped their second ATV and headed back down to O'Brien Creek on foot and looked for Mom by the water.

Travis and Chris heard ravens crying from below.

7750 unimproved Forest service road

After thoroughly searching the lower area, they once again climbed the 1.6 miles from O'Brien Creek, tediously but efficiently retracing their steps back to the meadow. Bennet Creek was another 2.25 miles down the road. That's where Mom and Dad had parted, and the ravens could be heard. And Detective Ash had theorized that Mom needed water and had to be confined to one of these canyons.

As they rounded the corner to the valley entrance, the pair heard flowing water. Travis took off down one side of Bennet Creek and Chris the other. They couldn't see each other through the thick brush as they winded along the stream.

They were 1.5 miles into the ravine when Travis yelled out to Chris, "I hear singing. Do you hear that?"

Chris couldn't hear well because of the creek, so he was going to make some smart aleck remark like "Yeah, you're hearing voices again." Suddenly, though, he heard Travis yelling, "We found her! We found her!"

Chris started running and busted through the thick brush. Both men stopped and stood in silence for a few moments, staring at the nude body, bees buzzing all over it. The woman—my mother—moved a little bit.

Startled, shock raced through them. They looked at each other in bewilderment and then back at the body.

"Holy cow, she's alive!" Chris squealed. He felt like jumping up and down.

Travis looked at his friend and shook his head in amazement. He motioned Chris to move in closer. They weren't expecting my mother to be alive. They were there to recover a body, yet there the "body" lay, mumbling something that sounded like nursery rhymes. She was lying there on her side against a log, about three feet from the stream. Her clothes were at her feet.

As the men approached my mother, they called out to her that they were from the sheriff's department. They took off their long-sleeved shirts and covered her body to keep away the yellow jackets that were feeding on her flesh.

"Boy, am I glad to see you! I'm ready to go home," she said.

"We're sure you are," Travis said.

"I want to go home and sleep in my own bed," she said longingly.

"Don't worry. We'll get you home," Chris assured her.

"Have you guys eaten lunch?" she asked in a humorous tone. "Are you paid enough to do this job?" It was just like my mother, even at such a low point, to think of others before herself when she hadn't eaten for two weeks.

Surprised by her sense of humor after all she had been through, the men laughed. She laughed too.

Travis looked at his friend and asked, "Will you be fine staying with her while I run up to radio the undersheriff and get some supplies?" The men were not prepared for a rescue.

Around 1:50 p.m., Travis took off running for better reception to radio for help and get the emergency blankets they had back at their four-wheeler. With so much adrenaline pumping, he made it all the way to the top of the drainage in eighteen minutes. He radioed Undersheriff Thompson, who was nearby in a service car, and gave him the GPS coordinates for the exact location.

The call came in at 2:08 p.m. The undersheriff radioed the

dispatcher, who subsequently radioed Sled Springs Rescue and Eagle Ambulance. The relay for my mother's life began, and each team player did his or her part to get Mom out of the woods.

Chris stayed with Mom and talked to her. It started sinking in how long she had been out there and in what circumstances. He thought, "Oh please just let her make it a little bit longer. We're almost there." How heartbreaking it would have been if she had survived that many days but didn't survive the rescue. As he wondered about her mental state, he asked her name.

Mom promptly rattled off her name, the year she was born, the name of her husband and two daughters, and our birth dates. Chris was surprised. Her body seemed to be dying, yet she was mentally alert.

It took nearly forty-five minutes for Travis to get back and announce that the rescue teams were on the way.

Meanwhile, the Baker County Sheriff's Department called Dad around 2:30 p.m. to say that Mom had been found.

"You mean you found her skeleton?" Dad asked. "What condition was it in?"

"No, she is alive!" The words rang like sweet music through his ears.

Dad jumped for joy. Cheryl received the good news, then called me and told me the authorities had found Mom alive! I screamed and then cried.

There is no way to describe the relief we all felt after being in the dark for so long. It was like getting Mom back from the dead. We didn't know much about what condition she was in, but she was alive!

A CELEBRATION
by Kristina Smith

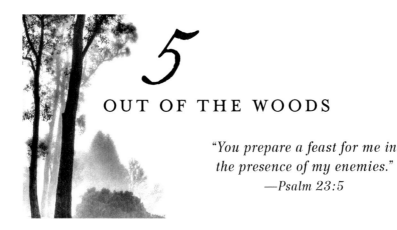

5
OUT OF THE WOODS

*"You prepare a feast for me in
the presence of my enemies."*
—Psalm 23:5

During the course of the workday at his regular job, Chris Galiszewski was listening to the police scanner radio traffic when the call came into dispatch that my mom had been found alive. The good news of Mom's survival spread quickly, as many who had been involved in the search efforts had been listening for updates on their scanners and rejoiced together because she was alive.

Galiszewski immediately went into action rounding up the necessary team members to get Mom out of the woods. Knowing the location was steep and brushy and that Mom needed immediate medical attention, he requested help from the US Forest Service Sled Springs helicopter repelling crew from the Umatilla National Forest Frazier base. The team players were Joseph Rodriguez, Ryan Miller, and Alan McKean, firefighters who rappel into rugged, remote areas to get to blazes. Also, Teruko Shibata, an emergency medical technician, boarded a flight to administer medical treatment until Mom was out of the woods.

Galiszewski also requested that Boise Life Flight be on standby at Two Colors Guard Station. Search and rescue and Eagle Valley Ambulance were alerted to head to the Bennet Creek Drainage.

Travis returned to Chris and Mom with blankets. They covered her and waited for the cavalry to show up. A law enforcement officer eventually arrived and flagged a trail, tying red tape on bushes to lead the rescue team to Mom. When the first helicopter showed up, it could not land because of the brush; it had to hover. Four firefighters rappelled down the hillside and lowered a stretcher to the ground.

Carlos Ramirez, part of the Forest Service team, asked Detective Ash and Trooper Hawkins, "Do you want a road? We can make you a road." A forest service member with a chainsaw as big as a Volkswagen bus cut them a road that a Mac truck could get through so they could carry Mom out.

At 4:20 p.m., search and rescue arrived. Shibata treated Mom's injuries; she was hypothermic, starving, dehydrated, and frostbitten. Search and rescue, Eagle Ambulance, and the firefighters who had rappelled down into the ravine carried Mom eight hundred yards uphill on a stretcher to an ambulance.

At 5:45 p.m., Mom was taken by ambulance to the Two Colors Guard Station. Next, Life Flight transported her to St. Elizabeth's Hospital in Baker City.

Mom landed at the hospital a little after 7:00 p.m. Dad, Cheryl, and I prepared to leave for Baker City around that same time. We were celebrating that she had been found alive.

We granted media interviews to three local TV stations before we left. We gladly shared our joy with the world. It felt as if Mom had risen from the dead.

Before we arrived in Baker City, *Good Morning America*, the *Today* show, and *The Early Show* were jockeying for position, bidding over who would get the story first. Agents for these shows wooed us, trying to convince us who would be the best morning program in America to break the news. They all wanted the first interview with the "Miracle Woman."

We pulled into the hospital parking lot around midnight. Media trucks filled the lot. The three local stations along with FOX, MSNBC, CNN, the *Today* show, *Good Morning America*, and *The Early Show* agents crowded outside plus representatives for the Associated Press, newspapers, and other publications such as *People* magazine as well as various radio stations. But we snuck into the hospital, leaving the reporters in the waiting room, who were excitedly waiting to share this good news with the world.

All of that was a mere distraction. We had only one desire, and that was to see Mom. Everything else could wait. I don't have words for what it felt like to see her. It was both wonderful and terrible at the same time.

Photo of Mom being carried out of the woods
(courtesy of Sandy Post)

Mom's Life flight (courtesy of Sandy Post)

She looked so old and shriveled. Her coloring was gray, but her face was sunburned and her lips were blistered. Sores covered her hands and arms as well as her lower body, feet, and legs. At some point, she lost her shoes, so her big toes were black from frostbite. Her dentures and glasses had also been lost during the ordeal.

It was heartbreaking to see her so weak and frail yet heartwarming to see her alive. Dad, Cheryl, and I had never seen her in such a weak condition. I could barely remember ever seeing her sick. Instead of my mom, I might have guessed she was my great-grandmother. She had lost weight—twenty pounds or more—and was skin and bones.

She mumbled, not seeming to recognize any of us. All we could do was sit with her and pray.

Her doctors and nurses focused on warming her up. Her core body temperature was ninety degrees when she was first brought in. They had never seen anyone with a core temperature as low as that who lived. I don't think she would have made it through another cold night. Fortunately, the heat from the sun that day had been on her side. Plus, she had been wrapped with wool blankets during the four hours it took to get her to the hospital.

When Mom first arrived in the emergency department, the medical team put her in a bear hugger to warm her. A bear hugger is a system that generates warm air, moving it through a tube into a thin plastic blanket. Warm air circulated through the plastic blanket that hugged her body.

The medical team did test after test on my mom, including checking her organs because she had reached the body temperature where they begin to shut down, coming and going from her room all night. No one really said much about Mom's condition; without knowing what the outcome would be, they were guarded but kind.

We never left Mom's bedside. We rested as much as possible in the chairs in the emergency room.

On the morning of Friday, September 7, the doctors classified Mom as being in critical condition. Mom had survived a lot already, and there was one thing I was sure of: she hadn't come that far to not make it all the way back home.

Detective Ash and Trooper Hawkins came to see Mom that morning. Sheriff Southwick and Undersheriff Thompson also came to visit and told us how happy they were she had been found. We got the pleasure of meeting members of the ambulance crew, one of the helicopter pilots, and others who were involved in the search and rescue. They were the only ones we allowed to see Mom at that time. There aren't words to adequately express our gratitude to all the people who contributed to saving her life. They're our heroes.

Later that afternoon, we finally did interviews with reporters who had camped out at the hospital and patiently waited to speak to us. What an experience that was. It had been a whirlwind of events and emotions since the initial storm had hit us. I had been spinning from the moment I had hung up the phone with dispatch at 4:00 a.m. on August 25, and fear had gripped me as I realized Mom was alone and afraid in such a vast wilderness. Then, on the fourteenth day, Mom was unexpectedly found alive. What a trip! Everyone who was involved in the case said the same thing: the story was unbelievable, unexplainable, and even miraculous.

Cheryl and I needed to get back to our kids, and my business couldn't run itself, but we were torn. None of us wanted Mom to be alone after all she had been through. The problem was that Dad, Cheryl, and I had ridden together from Dad's home in Sandy,

Oregon, to the hospital. Dr. Jon Schott, the emergency room doctor who had treated my mom, said he would find me a way home. Cheryl and Harvey could handle my business until I returned. Both Dad and Cheryl were comforted that I chose to stay with Mom. I believe Dad felt guilty for leaving Mom on the mountain, and it tore him up to see her in the condition she was in. Although I was glad to stay in Baker City with Mom until she could leave the hospital, I had not come prepared.

Once again, the kindness, helpfulness, and generosity of the people in Baker City amazed me. The Oregon Trail Motel & Restaurant donated a room and provided my meals as well as gifting me fifty dollars for personal needs. Pam Linderman even bought me a couple extra pairs of shoes. Every need I had was taken care of.

I spent the first evening at the hospital and got a ride to the motel with Melonie Matye, one of the emergency rooms nurses, when her shift ended.

On Saturday, September 8, my second day in Baker City, Jason Stein, an agent for *Good Morning America*, invited me to breakfast. The program wanted to do an interview about my mom's ordeal. Though I enjoyed meeting Jason, I had already accepted an offer from Art Swift, an agent for the *Today* show, to do an interview the next morning. Unfortunately, I couldn't satisfy Jason's request since both morning shows wanted the first interview. After breakfast, graciously, Jason dropped me off at the hospital.

When I entered Mom's room that morning, her eyes were wide open and she knew who I was. She said, "I'm so glad to see you. I was alone in the woods for a long time."

I hugged her and told her over and over again how much I loved her. These words, which had been held in my heart for weeks, now leaped out, grateful for the opportunity to be expressed. Tears welled up in my eyes and began to stream down my cheeks. Mom gently reached up her hand and wiped them away. At that moment, all was well because I had my mother back.

After I regained my composure, the first thing I told her was, "Mom, I really thought I would never see you again. Do you know that McKenna learned to tie her shoes and ride her bike? I've really wanted to tell you that. Mom, I'm so happy you're alive!"

I had no trouble trying to find words to say. I spent the day telling my mom the unsaid things from my mental list and was glad for the chance to do so.

"What was it like out there?" I asked her at one point during our conversation.

"Well, I'm not going back to the forest; there are no burger joints there." She said it as though the forest was to be crossed off her list of places to eat.

She was lighthearted and funny at times. She joked with her nurses, holding up both arms and showing off her sores. "Hey, look at this. I have a polka-dotted arm and another one to match." The nurses laughed, and Mom was enjoying the warmth of other people.

On the serious side, Mom said, "As I lay on the forest floor and looked up, I saw bears in the forks of the trees."

"No way! Bears?" I shrieked. "You're scared to death of bears." I was stunned by what she told me.

"Uh-huh. Do you know bears are silent when they walk?" she asked, looking me right in the eyes.

"What? Bears were that close to you? Oh my goodness, it really is a miracle that you lived." I hugged and kissed her again—as a matter of fact, I showered her with hugs and kisses all day. She was still in critical condition, but we had a wonderful day together.

Cards and flowers with goodwill wishes continued to pour into Mom's hospital room along with baskets of fruit, strawberries and chocolate, meat, cheese, and crackers. Dad and Cheryl had taken home a basket, yet we were still able to feed a good part of the hospital staff the extra.

Phone calls kept coming from media everywhere. Even Jay Leno sent his regards. Dad and Cheryl called and checked in, too.

I spent all day with Mom, talking with her and eating from the food baskets. There was even my favorite candy: Lindt chocolate truffles with the melt-in-your-mouth center—yum! I was eating some of the truffles when I heard Mom say something so incredible I nearly choked. "Did you say mother bear and cubs? Wait, back up and tell me that again," I told her.

She told me the story about her first night out in the woods. I was on the edge of my seat as she described the details: "Well, I had laid down on the bank near the stream, and I had fallen asleep on the leaves. When I woke up, it was dark. I remember walking up the stream, and the moonlight was shining on her."

"Her?" I asked.

"I saw the mother bear. She was sitting on a tree limb, and her three little cubs were on the ground under her. They were sleeping." She paused. "It's a good thing the moon was shining or I wouldn't have seen them."

"What did you do?"

"Well, I didn't check to see if she was awake, if that's what you mean," she said, teasing me.

"No, Mom, really."

"I quietly turned around and went back downstream. I'm so glad to be out of those woods."

I came undone when I heard that story. I kissed Mom good night and headed for the motel and restaurant. I needed to process all I had learned.

At the restaurant, my waitress brought my order to the table and, after realizing who I was and who my mother was, told me she had woken up one night when the authorities were searching for my mom and looked out her window at the mountains, thinking of my mom out there in the cold and dark. Moved with compassion, the waitress had stayed up and prayed for my mom. The fact that someone who didn't know my mom would care enough about her to pray for her instead of sleeping made a big impact on me.

It turned out that God had called an army of people from all over the world, moved by Mom's story in the news to pray for her.

While at the restaurant that night, I met Sally Selson, owner of the Baker City Taxi Company. She offered me free rides anywhere in the city limits as long as I was in town. I experienced how high, wide, and deep God's love is through the kindness of these people.

BY THE LIGHT OF THE MOON
by Steve De Jesus Olivares

6

DELIVERED FROM FEAR

"You honor me by anointing my head with oil. My cup overflows with blessings."
—*Psalm 23:5*

On Sunday, September 9, I got up at 4:00 a.m. and made my best attempt to look beautiful and did a three-minute interview with the *Today* show. The filming was done in front of St. Elizabeth's Hospital. The biting cold grieved me as I thought about what my mom had gone through. How could she have lasted so long in that cold?

Amy Dunkak, then St. Elizabeth's director of communications, had helped me set up for the interview. I developed a special bond with Amy and enjoyed our conversations. It's no wonder she was the hospital's communications director because our conversations made me feel like I'd gained another sister.

She arranged for me to go to Barbara Jeans clothing, a shop in Baker City. (I find this especially amusing because my name is Barbara Jean.) The owner, a friend of Amy's, opened the store early and let me pick out a few outfits, as I expected more interviews to come. The people of Baker City gave me celebrity-worthy treatment.

After the interview, Amy dropped me off at the motel. As soon as I got into my room, the hospital called to tell me Mom was having trouble, and they needed me to get there as soon as possible. Thank God for the free taxi service. The taxi pulled up to the curb, and I thanked the driver and rushed to Mom's room.

Mom scowled at me from her hospital bed as I walked in. "Look what they have done to me!" She held out her arms.

"Do you know how you got those sores, Mom?"

"Yes, I do," she said, agitated. "These people." She pointed to the hospital staff.

"Mom, it's okay. No one here has hurt you," I said in the gentlest tone I could muster.

"Who are you?" she asked, staring at me blankly. "I want to go. Can I leave now?"

My heart sank. "It's me, Barbara, your daughter. Don't you recognize me?"

"No, I don't think so," she sneered, shaking her head as if she wasn't going to let me pull anything over on her.

"Mom, you can't leave the hospital. You need to lie back down. Your feet and legs are swelling." Mom's legs had been elevated ever since she had arrived at the hospital to reduce the swelling. They had made a tent to keep even the sheet from touching her frostbitten toes. Her legs now looked like they had swollen to at least twice their normal size. The sores were oozing, and she was obviously in pain.

Two of her nurses, trying to help encourage her to lie back down, spoke softly to her: "Mrs. Anderson, you must rest."

But Mom wouldn't cooperate, so the three of us tried to coerce her to stay in bed. Two of us gently forced her down on her back while the other one lifted her dangling feet and legs back onto the bed.

"No!" she screamed, stretching out the word.

Mom had resisted us, screaming and fuming the whole time, but at least we managed to get her to lie back down in her bed where she needed to be.

Fighting back the tears, I whispered to the nurse, "Can she be sedated?"

The nurse left to find the doctor to prescribe some medication to calm Mom down until she got through this.

After the nurses left, my mom looked at me with cold, piercing eyes. "I just want to die. I want to be twelve feet under." Never before had I heard my mother talk this way.

I suddenly realized who was speaking for my mom; fear and worry had finally come out of hiding and were showing themselves. Her enemies were trying to take over, and death had now joined them. They wanted her dead. Demons were manifesting.

I didn't take time to discuss things with my mother's enemies; I knew what to do and began binding and casting the demons out of my mom. I declared to them and to her that she would live and not die.

The nurse returned and sedated her. All day long I continued casting demons out of my mom. Strangely, she pursed her lips and blew out even as she slept throughout the day as I continued this deliverance and released healing into her mind and body. Afterward, she slept hard.

I was glad she was sleeping because I, too, was exhausted. I had been fighting all day for my mom, battling a spiritual war with her enemies.

I left Mom's hospital room and met Joe Rose, a reporter for the *Oregonian*. Despite being tired and upset, I tried to remain positive and be friendly.

Seemingly endless calls still came in from various media. Prior to my mom's episode, I was so excited about the upcoming interview with *Good Morning America* planned for the following day, September 10. I even had a new outfit to wear but, considering the change in circumstances, I was not looking forward to the interview any longer. I didn't have any good news to share. However, Jason Stein wound up calling me and telling me the interview had been canceled. I was so relieved.

That night, before I went to bed, my friend Tom Butel joined me on the phone, and we prayed for my mom's freedom. It was powerful, and I knew there were many others joined with us as we took authority, released our faith, and declared God's Word bringing down the rain of heaven. I had peace and slept well.

The next morning when I saw my mom, she knew who I was. She looked at me, smiling, and said in the sweet, soft voice I recognized, "You know, I thought I saw you yesterday, but I guess I was dreaming. I cried out to the Lord to help me and you know what? He did. He just woke me up this morning. I am so happy to be alive! I was not ready to die."

I smiled at her, joy and thankfulness welling up inside me. "Good morning, Mom. I'm glad too."

All day Mom stayed wide awake and alert. She didn't need sedation. It was quite interesting to see the surprise and delight on the faces of all the hospital staff who had worked with Mom and witnessed her traumatic episode the previous day.

Diane Bean, her night nurse, slugged me in the arm. "Wow," she said, "she is a night-and-day difference."

Diana Downing, the physical therapist who had worked with Mom the day before, told me, "I can't believe this is the same woman I saw yesterday."

Doctors and other staff members echoed the same sentiments throughout the day at the change in my mom's condition.

My mom's former companions, the enemies fear and worry, no longer had control over her mind to influence and distort her thinking. Fear, worry, and death lost their power and had left her. My family couldn't have known that the Lord would use Satan's plan to destroy Mom to actually free her. Just as David, a shepherd boy, rescued the sheep from the mouth of the lion and bear, the Lord, my mom's shepherd, rescued her from bears, worry, and the jaws of fear and death.

Since 1993, I have been a committed follower of Jesus Christ. I have always believed but got serious about it then. I read the Bible all the way through for the first time and have read it each year since. My mom, a believer from the time she was a small child, hadn't been free from trouble in this world. Some trouble comes from our own choices or weaknesses; some comes through generational issues.

An explanation of this can be found in Deuteronomy 30:19: "Today I have given you the choice between life and death, between blessings and curses. Now I call on heaven and earth to witness the choice you make. Oh, that you would choose life, so that you and your descendants might live." "We are not fighting against flesh-and-blood enemies, but against evil rulers and authorities of the unseen world, against mighty powers in the dark world, and against evil spirits in the heavenly places."[5]

Our enemies look for weakness, sin, or disobedience to God that creates open doors. They prey on our weaknesses and thrive on the strength of our flesh or mind, will, and emotions (our soul.) That being said, demons can build a stronghold or fortress in the mind is not easily taken down. Their influence binds, distorts, and

esians 6:12

directs the thoughts and actions of the mind held captive. Since we are not in medieval times, a more modern way to explain strongholds is wrong thinking. "Jesus called his twelve disciples together and gave them authority to cast out evil spirits and to heal every kind of disease and illness" (Matthew 10:1). He also tells His disciples "to heal the sick, raise the dead, cure those with leprosy, and cast out demons" and to "give as freely as you have received" (Matthew 10:8).

A disciple is someone who follows Jesus. I believe everything God's Word says because, from practical experience, He has proven to be faithful and trustworthy to me. I believe He created us and has all the answers. I have both knowledge and experience in deliverance.

An explanation for why my mom pursed her lips and was blowing out all day is that demons, when they are cast out, leave in the form of yawns, breathing out, coughing, or even vomiting. They're spirit, which means breath, so they come out in breaths. I believe they all came out while Mom was sleeping.

HE RESCUED ME (AN INTERPRETATION OF PSALM 18:16-17)
by Steve DeJesus Olivares

Mom when she was young.

Dad, feeling victorious! (Picture courtesy of the Sandy Post)

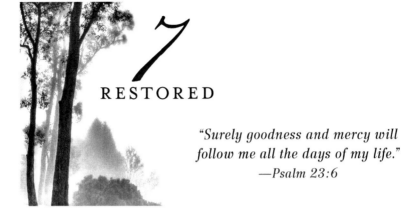

7

RESTORED

*"Surely goodness and mercy will
follow me all the days of my life."*
—*Psalm 23:6*

L ife is a journey with a series of mountains and valleys to cross. Every dip and turn leads to new things to discover and experience. My mom had made it through the wilderness, out of her dark valley, and off the mountain, yet she still had a ways to go before she could come all the way home.

The first step for Mom to leave St. Elizabeth's and make her journey home was restoring her dentures. Mom had lost her teeth in the woods, and this was a problem because she couldn't return to eating solid food without them. Mom had been without food for fourteen days, and it was a slow process introducing solids back into her system. The dieticians and Dr. Schott designed a feeding plan that began with intravenous feeding and then special TPN protein shakes.

I remember one day asking Dr. Schott whether she could just have some mashed potatoes or ice cream because I wanted her to enjoy it. He knew it might have been too soon but gave in against his better judgment to a few treats. She enjoyed the ice cream so much, it was as if she was experiencing it for the first time.

"Yum, that's so good. Can I have more?" she asked.

It was so much fun watching Mom eat, but an hour later, it was not fun for her nurses. Mom's system couldn't handle the ice cream, so it was back to the slow and steady plan.

Elkhorn Denture Service of Baker City found out my mother had lost her teeth and came to the hospital, molded her mouth, and made her a set of dentures. To my amazement, the denturist accomplished in one day what would normally take a week or longer. Then, to top it off, the service gifted her with the beautiful new set of teeth.

Dr. Schott kept his promise when he said he would get me back home from Baker City. He arranged to have Mom and I flown back to the Portland Airport between the wings of an angel—Angel Flight, that is. Angel Flight is a nonprofit charitable organization created by a group of pilots to bless individuals and health care organizations by volunteering to provide free air transportation for medical-related needs. They even use their own planes.

The trip to Portland was remarkable in several ways. First, there was the absence of fear and worry in my mom. In the past, she would have been afraid to fly. Dr. Schott asked her before we left the hospital for the airport if she would like a sedative for the flight.

"No, there is nothing to be afraid of," she told him. This was extremely out of character for my mom, especially since the plane we were flying in was a small four-passenger aircraft.

It was a perfect flight, sunny with beautiful, clear-blue sky, and Mom was completely at peace.

When we landed, an ambulance transport company met us at the Portland Airport and took us to Providence Hospital, where Mom stayed for about a month of therapy and recovery. A lot of media attention surrounded this.

At that time, my family still had our guard up because we'd experienced such a whirlwind of events, and we were tired. There had been pressure about interviewing Mom and pressure about who would get the first interview. As a family, our main concern was Mom and Dad's recovery and well-being.

Dad got pretty wrapped up in the media attention for quite some time. He actually wanted to sneak Mom out of the hospital for a television interview he had committed to. Providence Hospital, though, had a locked-down security system; every door was monitored, so Mom was ensured privacy. My family simply wanted things to calm down for Mom and Dad so they could adjust to all the changes. We wanted them to rest without feeling pressured.

Nonetheless, it was still a pretty difficult time for us as a family. Dad was stressed because Mom couldn't come home. We all had a lot of travel time to and from the hospital for visiting. After the high of getting Mom back, the process from recovery to restoration was challenging

After Mom received all the necessary care from Providence Hospital, she was moved to Marquis Centennial in Portland, Oregon. The rehabilitation center where my mom would finish her therapy and regain her strength was about an hour's drive from my parents' home. Her care team's goal was to help Mom return to the self-sufficiency she had before her wilderness experience. First, Mom had to be able to stand, then progress to walking again.

After two months of hard work and great care, Mom came home. My parents did an interview with the *Today* show from their home in Sandy, Oregon.

Fame lasts for a moment but good news, a good story, lasts forever. I had asked the Lord to restore my mom and bring her home, and He did. I had asked the Lord to deliver Mom from fear and worry, and He did.

For more than seven years, I asked the Lord to restore my family. I asked for freedom from bondage as well as emotional, mental, and physical wholeness for all my family members. I asked for jubilee, which is all of that plus debt cancellation. My family has some debts to pay, and it would not be okay with us to leave this world owing anyone anything except to love them. I believe my family's journey through the wilderness and out of the valley of death ultimately will lead us to our Promised Land.

The Lord gave me a good story to tell and the gift of telling it. My hope is that the freedom I have spoken of is transmitted to all who need it.

Jesus said, "The Spirit of the Lord is on me, because he has anointed me to preach good news to the poor. He has sent me to proclaim freedom to the prisoners and recovery of sight for the blind, to release the oppressed, to proclaim the year of the Lord's favor."[6] Jesus proclaimed liberation from sin and all its consequences.

The foundation of jubilee is found in Leviticus 25:9–10: "Then have the trumpet sounded everywhere on the tenth day of the seventh month; on the Day of Atonement sound the trumpet

---

6   Isaiah 61:1–

throughout your land. Consecrate the fiftieth year and proclaim liberty throughout the land to all its inhabitants. It shall be a jubilee for you."

There's nothing in life I value more than my family and our freedom. I want what God's Word promises we can have. I took hold of these promises on August 29, 2004. I wrote out a debt cancellation agreement using God's Word.

His Word remains the same yesterday, today, and forever: "God says He is not a man so he does not lie."[7] His angels listen to His Word to perform it.

The Lord showed me that this promise of freedom and restoration was not just for me but for anyone who believes. Eighteen people, including my mom and dad, entered into this agreement and signed it. As I write this, it's almost seven years later. Seven is a number of completion, of perfection. I can only say once again that God has proved He is faithful.

I've discovered time after time the reward of faith, which is why I love and trust God completely. I've shared about this specific request I made to God for this reason. As I was going back over each day of this story, it suddenly hit me that September 10, the seventh month and tenth day, by the Hebrew calendar, the day of freedom, of jubilee when the trumpets sounded, was the day Mom woke up in her right mind. She was delivered from her bondage of fear and worry; Jesus opened her prison doors and set her free. That day screamed faithfulness to me because I had studied it. My family had trusted Him, embraced Him, and believed He would work things out to our benefit. It wasn't a coincidence that God fulfilled His word, His promise, His blood covenant, our agreement at that time.

First I cried, and then I was filled with joy because He is so faithful and because even though He is the God of the whole universe, He wants a personal, intimate relationship with each of us. He wants to be our greatest love, friend, manager, owner, and shepherd. But first we need to be restored and belong to Him. My family is so grateful that we belong to Him.

The intimacy that we have with him is so beautiful. Overwhelming joy wells up in our souls, making us want to sing, shout, and dance!

---

7   Numbers 23:19

That's worship: an expression of all the emotion and gratitude that makes you feel like bursting with joy.

The Israelites had a huge celebration and rejoiced in their freedom at the time of their jubilee festival. My family is bursting with joy. We're going to spend each day we have in an attitude of celebration, thankfulness, and gratefulness because God's love, goodness, and mercy are great. We're also going to spend the rest of our days spreading this good news and extending that same love, goodness, and mercy to everyone we can. We've learned that when you're having a hard time and someone extends goodness and mercy to you, it's like a breath of life.

We're for life. Our God wants to restore life and freedom to all who are lost and need to come all the way home.

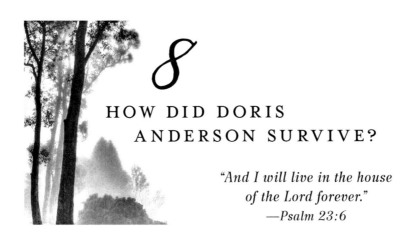

8

HOW DID DORIS ANDERSON SURVIVE?

"And I will live in the house
of the Lord forever."
—Psalm 23:6

The world has been asking this question since my mom was found alive in northeastern Oregon's Wallowa Mountains. By the end of her ordeal, Mom had survived fourteen days without shelter, protection, or food. How?

At seventy-six, my mother was out in the elements from August 24 through September 6, 2007, wearing only light clothing. Several storms swept through the mountains during that period. Wild animals, specifically cougars and bears, lived in the remote, dangerous terrain. Mom had no gear and no communication devices to call for help. Detective Travis Ash and Trooper Chris Hawkins did find a pair of tweezers next to her, but they probably weren't helpful in her survival.

What did my mom eat during those fourteen days? Travis and Chris think she ate crabapples. The snow melted early, and the huckleberries had already come and gone by the time Mom was in the woods, so she probably didn't eat those. She drank water from Bennet Creek, next to where she was found.

Mom doesn't remember a lot of details from those days, though she does remember the bears. I was talking with her about how bears stink from having smelled them at the zoo. She said she knew when they were near because she could smell them, and she would avoid the area.

Another detail she remembers is the sound of cougars screaming in the night. I can only imagine the fear she must have experienced.

Mom also said there were animals in her bed, though we're not sure what. The officers said cows were in the meadow and down in the valley. The ranchers let their cattle open-range graze in the alpine meadows and hillsides on US Forest Service land, so she may have seen Black Angus cows. Chris thought maybe Mom mistook the cows for bears except she knows that cows don't sleep in trees.

Many parts of this picture needed to be filled in. I started to write this book right after Mom and I got back home from Baker City in 2007. I knew someday I would go and experience the place where my mom had been. I was compelled to do this.

With my friends Karen and Darcy Lais

On the one-year anniversary of my parents' misadventure, I got the opportunity to go explore the Wallowas. My friend Karen Lais and her husband, Darcy, went with me. Darcy, a fireman, made me feel safer. He was also an experienced outdoorsman who loved to hunt, camp, and fish. Unlike me, he knew how to read maps.

Karen, like me, loves to talk, and she and I have a heart connection and are like sisters. She and her husband were the perfect companions for the trip, my fellow detectives as we unraveled the mysteries.

Chris, Darcy, and I at the campground getting
ready to follow Chris to Bennet Creek

Darcy at our campground where we spent our first night

We met Chris in Baker City on August 23, 2008, and followed him into the snowcapped Eagle Mountain Wilderness. It was as beautiful as I had been told.

Chris took us to the campground where we would stay that first night. Chris said Bennet Creek wasn't far. Even though there wasn't much daylight left, he could take us the rest of the way if we wanted to go. Mom had spent so much time in the dark, so I wanted to experience a taste of what she went through.

The territory blew us away; it was so rugged, high, and remote.

As we followed Chris on the rough, steep road, I couldn't imagine my mom there alone. "Man, when you're talking about isolation, you can't get much more isolated than this," I said to Karen and Darcy as we viewed the area for the first time.

Karen burst out in amazement, "It's just this huge canyon! Do you see that? Like a deep hole and mountains on the other side. This is the valley of the shadow of death, even in the way it looks."

"Oh my gosh, it's deep. I can't even see down there!" I gasped.

It was dark when we arrived at Bennet Creek at 8:30 p.m.

"Is this the ravine?" I asked Chris.

"This is the drainage. You can't see the creek here, but if you listen, it's right down in there," he said, pointing in the direction of the canyon, "and when you go up around the corner, you can really hear it."

"I can hear the creek," I said. "I've been standing out here for maybe a minute, and I'm shivering."

"Yeah, and the temperature's going to be the same if not cooler than it was when your mom was here," Chris said.

"In the thirties?" Karen asked.

"At night, yeah, it could be in the thirties. During the day, it's nice and warm—shorts and T-shirt weather—but at night it cools off fast," Chris told us.

"What is the elevation right here?" I asked.

After checking his GPS, Chris said, "The elevation's 5,280 feet."

Soon, it was pitch-black—dark enough that you couldn't see your hand in front of your face.

"So, Chris, does the meadow stay flat and then just drop off into the canyon?" I asked

Chris and I shivering in the dark at Bennet Creek

"Well, if someone was going to walk down here, this would be the spot. As you begin walking down, it's kind of wide, then it starts getting narrower, the sides get steeper, and then it funnels down into the creek."

I walked away from the others for a few moments to be alone with my thoughts. The darkness overwhelmed me. I realized standing there in the cold and dark that this was beyond my ability to understand. I would never grasp what Mom went through. All the mixed emotions shook me: gratefulness that she was rescued yet horror over what a serious, dangerous, and isolated place the wilderness had been.

That night, I slept outdoors in a sleeping bag. The cold pierced through the layers, and the dark shrouded the area. Mom didn't remember being cold. Perhaps God, in His mercy, took that memory away from her.

The next morning, Chris and Travis came to our campsite, and we all headed for the spot of the first traumatic event. Travis and Chris retold the events of the story as they knew it. My friends and I then got back in our SUV and followed Travis and Chris on the way to our next clue.

"Well, that's important. That's where it all began: at the junction of 7750 and 025," Darcy said.

"Yeah, your dad broke his wrist and maybe hurt his head, and that's why he took the wrong road," Karen said.

Nodding his head in agreement, Darcy said, "It's all starting to make sense how it could have happened."

Travis and Chris ready to take us on an adventure

Where it all began

Travis and Chris tell us the story.

Discussing what happened

Two Colors Camp Area and two roads to choose

I had asked Darcy to drive my SUV so I could focus on the adventure instead of driving.

"Can you imagine trying to drive on this road with a broken wrist and trailer?" he asked. We were on the same rough road we had been on the night before when we had followed Chris.

"I remember how grieved I was for my dad. His trip turned disastrous from the beginning—all the planning and money he spent, and he didn't get to enjoy anything," I said.

We were just a few miles in to our drive when Karen asked, "You have a flat tire?"

"Yep," Darcy answered.

We changed the tire quickly but were further delayed because my steering wheel locked up. After an hour of determination, we were finally on our way. The mishap confirmed how hard it was to travel on that rocky road. I was told the land had been cursed by the Indians who used to live here.

Glad to be moving again, we followed Travis and Chris another four miles to the log where the Buckmaster hunting party had found Dad.

The log marks the spot where Dad was found on August 25, 2007.

"Gosh, he went a long ways up this road. Wasn't there a spot he could have turned around?" I asked Travis.

"Several, but not with the trailer," Travis answered. "He was in shock; that's what I'm thinking. That's the only thing that would explain it, the only theory I could come up with as to why he would come so far down this road."

We passed Bennet Creek 1.5 miles down the 7750 forest service road and then continued traveling the 8.25-mile detour, veering off at O'Brien Creek.

I imagined how hard it must have been for Dad and how nervous and scared Mom must have felt so far away from civilization. We reached a point where the road grew too rough to drive my vehicle, and Chris asked if we wanted to ride with them.

"Let's walk so we don't beat them up too bad," Travis decided.

Travis and Chris walked us the rest of the way to where Mom and Dad's vehicle had gotten stuck. "Knowing my mom, if she had to walk back here to the truck, she would have been totally freaked out to be left here alone," I said.

"Anybody would be all by themselves. You saw how dark it was last night with the stars," Chris said.

"Is this some of that red marking tape?" Chris asked Travis, speaking of the red ribbon that remained tied on the bushes. Travis nodded his head yes.

"Ah! How would you turn around here with the trailer?" I said, viewing the steep, narrow spot, perplexed by the dilemma my dad had faced.

We discussed all the issues my parents had encountered and concluded that it had been impossible to get out any other way except on foot.

"It's hot out here," I said, wiping the sweat off my brow.

"Just wait a few hours," Chris said.

I told Travis and Chris that the newspaper reported the temperature had risen to between 82.6 and 85.9 degrees during the time when my parents had been here. "Do you remember what the temperature was like?" I asked.

The tape marks the spot where Mom
and Dad's vehicle was stranded.

Chris recalled being in Burns, Oregon, at the time, which is five hours southeast from where we were. Chris said it had been even hotter in the Wallowas. He told us, "We were in T-shirts, and it was hotter than a pistol."

After we started climbing out, I tired quickly because of the steepness and heat. Abandoning my plan and changing my mind, I said, "Well, I was going to walk from here, but I don't think I necessarily have to."

Karen, in agreement, said, "Yeah, I'm not going to."

Happy I didn't have to walk, I climbed back into the truck. We drove another 1.6 miles up the hill and got out at the meadow where Mom and Dad had napped.

"This is the meadow where they took a rest," Travis said.

"Were they under that tree in the shade where the red tape is tied?" I asked. "It would make sense because of the straight-up climb in the hot sun."

"I would have taken a nap too. I like naps," Travis said, laughing. Any of us would have felt like a nap after that climb.

"This is also the place where we heard the ravens crying the day we found your mom," Chris said, moving closer to the ridge and pointing down in the direction of Bennet Creek Drainage.

My excitement was building as we drove on since there were only a few more miles to Bennet Creek.

We pulled off the road and prepared to enter what was the valley of the shadow of death for my mom.

I planned to spend a night in the dark canyon like my mom had. I wanted to experience what it may have been like for her. I could surely handle one night if Karen and Darcy were with me. After all, I trusted God to take care of me.

Before we started walking down the canyon, I said to Travis, "I just want to tell you how much I appreciate this because it really means a lot to me to be able to see what they went through. My mom is certainly tougher than I ever gave her credit for."

"Yeah, I'll never complain about being cold as far as being out and stuff. I tell myself, 'Nope, I'm not cold. I've got a coat,'" Travis said and then warned us, "It's brushy down there. Get ready for 'buggies.'"

"Do you mean mosquitoes?" I asked.

Tape tied to the tree in meadow where my parents napped

At the entrance of the ravine

"No, mostly bees and flies."

We began talking about cows, bears, cougars, and other animals that lived in the area. We had probably taken five steps into the meadow when Travis pointed out, "Wow, looks like a bear worked over that log there."

"Okay, so point out what a bear tunnel is if you see one. I was told by the rescue team there were bear tunnels in this valley," I said.

"See all those broken branches and that stump? A bear did that," Chris said.

"Do you know that was done by a bear because you're a hunter or a fish and game guy or what?" I asked.

"Probably from hunting with my dad," Chris said.

"Bear evidence" littered the meadow going into the valley. Chris pointed out a bear tunnel, trodden-down brush about the width of the bear resembling a tunnel. He said there also were caves, but he couldn't point out one.

Chris showed us bear damage, such as the pawed-up logs, broken branches, and scratched-up trees. Karen wondered whether cows had done the damage since ranchers were allowed to let their cows graze on the forest service land. Chris and Travis told us cows had been in the valley when my mom was there, and the grass was much shorter then. I knew Karen hoped the damage we saw was from cows.

"No," Chris insisted, pointing out evidence, such as a bear's paw prints and bear poop. Both big and little bear poop lay everywhere. Mom had survived in the "living room" of the three little bears. Unfortunately, they had no porridge or beds for her.

The walk in was pretty easy once Karen and I got past our fear of bears. It helped that Travis and Chris had guns. I couldn't help but think that Mom didn't have a gun when she was lost.

As we went down the stream, it became swampy. My shoes filled with water and muck. Had Mom's shoes come off in the muck? I wondered.

We wound down through the brush toward the spot where Travis and Chris had found my mom. We followed the trail the Forest Service crew cut when they had brought her out. It was a little overgrown yet a good path to hike on.

Bear poo

The brush

The trail

Chris looked at his watch. "Dang near on the dot the time when we started down here last year," he said.

I was actually retracing Mom's steps at the same time on the same day a year later. Mom and Dad spent the night of August 23, 2007, in their truck and walked out the next morning, August 24. I had done nothing to manipulate the time or date I made this trip; the weekend of August 23 and 24 just happened to be open and work best with everyone's schedules. To find myself walking this path on August 24, 2008, at the same time confirmed for me that I was at the right place and time for a reason.

"I see what you meant about a funnel, Chris," I said. "You're right; the canyon walls get narrower and steeper as you go."

Chris pointed toward the bottom of the canyon. "Water cascades straight off the canyon walls way down in the bottom." Then he pointed up and showed us where he and Travis had come down halfway on the other side of the canyon when they first heard the ravens. "We were right up in that ridge. You know hindsight's 20/20. If we would've walked straight down the hill, we would've been right on top of her."

The men had been at the top of the ridge when they heard ravens.

Travis pointed out the place about a mile in where he'd heard singing. The way was thick with brush and rocky ground. Just around the corner, we reached the point where Travis first saw my mom. The bank dropped off directly into the creek and sheer, steep canyon walls narrowed and surrounded it like a trap. We waded across the creek, and then Travis showed me where he had found Mom.

Dropping off into the creek

She was lying right next to the stream by a log. There was red tape still tied there to mark the spot. I lay on the ground in the spot where Mom had been so Karen could take pictures.

Travis and Chris showing me where they found Mom

Lying in the spot where Mom was found

"Her head was downhill," Travis told me.

I got into the same position as she had been. Branches poked me on the hard ground. On that hot day, it felt muggy there by the stream.

As I lay there, the Lord spoke to me. "She was dying." I told Chris and Travis what I heard.

"We saw it," Travis said.

"No question about that," Chris agreed, mentioning his cousin, who's a doctor, had told him all the heat goes to the body's core, and that's the last stage of hypothermia. When a person strips off his or her clothing, the end is near. The person will die without intervention. I knew the Lord had sent Travis and Chris just in time.

Travis and Chris showed me an area under some trees near the spot where Mom was found that was a little protected. They believed she had spent the majority of the days she had been missing there based on the evidence that was found. Too weak and tired to go back out of the ravine, Mom probably hadn't left the area once.

**The area where Travis and Chris think Mom spent
most of her fourteen days in the wilderness**

The guys pulled me out of the creek bed. I had grabbed on to vines and branches to try to pull myself up, but I couldn't. The pitch was too steep and the ground too soft to get any footing.

My senses swam from all the sights, sounds, emotions, and information flooding in. I wanted to hike around and explore everything. Mom had lost her shoes, dentures, glasses, and purse with Dad's keys. Undersheriff Thompson looked around after Mom had been rescued and didn't find anything. Karen, Darcy, and I hoped to recover the missing items. However, I was aware of the time Travis and Chris had taken out of their weekend, and I didn't want to keep them longer than necessary. Since Karen, Darcy, and I planned to come back down and camp out anyway, maybe we would find something Mom lost when we returned. We looked around a little then headed back up.

Karen videotaped much of the trip, including me talking with Travis and Chris. The pair was struck by the fact that a lot of things had to come together for Mom's rescue to happen. Travis was supposed to be somewhere else on September 6: he had an arrest warrant to serve in Washington, but the plans fell through. Chris also was scheduled to be somewhere else that day, but his path was changed as well. I believe the Lord redirected their paths because Mom didn't have any more time.

And what made Undersheriff Thompson wait on Eagle Road that day at noon? Travis, Chris, and the undersheriff came back out looking to recover a body. It took five hours to get Mom to the hospital. Would Mom have survived if Thompson had not been out there to receive the radio call and dispatch for help so fast?

Both men told me they dreamed about finding my mom for two weeks after the rescue. Being neighbors, they had each other to process the impact that finding her had on them.

Travis told about shouting out to Chris over his backyard fence: "Hey, Chris, have you been having dreams? Are you seeing Doris a lot?"

"Yeah, you too?"

Chris mentioned he had seen a lot of bad things in his years as an officer that visited him in the night but not like this. It seemed like whenever there was a quiet moment, the picture of finding Mom replayed in his mind. Neither he nor Travis had experienced anything like that before.

"It felt so good. It was, 'Man, I can't believe we found her!'" Chris said, glancing back at Travis. "This happened on the heels of someone who didn't make it half as long, so you don't expect this type of stuff."

"I dreamed about finding her," Travis said. "I kept seeing her and hearing the rotors from the helicopters." He shook his head. "Maybe it impacted us so strongly because we weren't prepared to find her alive."

My mother's story defied science and all odds. "I'm happy about the publicity you got for finding Mom," I said.

"It was good news for law enforcement," Travis said.

Travis and Chris both received the Harold R. Berg Lifesaving Award, a high honor for the state of Oregon's law enforcement, for their perseverance and dedication in looking for Mom one more time after all other efforts had failed. That extra degree of effort saved my mom's life. They also received a Top Cops Award, recognizing their above-and-beyond efforts from National Law Enforcement for outstanding service, delivered by John Walsh, the host of *America's Most Wanted*.

We reached the top of the canyon and got back in our vehicles. Travis and Chris drove away. I would forever be grateful and never forget them.

Karen, Darcy, and I got lawn chairs out of my Nissan Xterra and sat awhile, discussing how we felt about going back into the valley and staying overnight. Both Karen and Darcy would've done whatever I wanted, but I no longer felt like it was necessary. I thought I had gotten the information that I came for.

Also, now that Travis and Chris were gone with their guns, I really didn't want to go back into the bears' home. I'd been so determined about experiencing what Mom had for one night, but now the thought of spending the night in the pitch-black surrounded by black bears scared me. Even knowing how the Lord protected my mom all the time she was in that dark valley, I had faith but felt fear.

Prior to this trip, I had imagined Mom falling into the ravine. It was the only thing that made sense to me as to why she couldn't get out. She must have been unconscious since she didn't respond to all the searchers calling her name. I had questions, such as why didn't Mom walk out the same way she went in?

Karen, Darcy, and I prayed for revelation and the gaps began to fill in. Mom must've had a breakdown, been scared out of her mind, and hidden.

Darcy unpacking our chairs after our climb out of the canyon

How small is a human in relation to this environment?

Chris had confirmed it when he told me Mom said an officer had shot Dad and he had fallen off the ATV. Maybe this thought came from the image of him hanging upside down when she freed him.

Chris had asked Mom if she heard anyone calling her name. "Oh, yes," she replied. "But I didn't answer because it was the people that shot my husband."

Chris thought her mind played tricks on her because of fear, starvation, and the length of exposure to the cold and dark. If she had been hiding, Chris said he would have pretty much needed to step on her to find her.

When I was planning to spend the night there, Chris told me to expect a lot of noises I couldn't identify. The wilderness is a whole different experience than living in the suburbs. "Once in a while you hear a jet to remind you that you're still in civilization, but other than that, it's wilderness." Chris doubted even he could make it two weeks.

I realized later that evening as I sat by the campfire trying to figure out what had happened to my mom that three of my friends had given me clues. The first piece to the puzzle came from my friend Susan; she gave me Psalm 18 when Mom was first lost. The second piece came from my friend Kimi when she handed me an envelope that contained a card with a verse from Psalm 18 when I dropped off my daughter McKenna while I went on the trip to the Wallowas. The third piece came from Karen as we were on the road heading for the Wallowas. All three pieces were Psalm 18.

I was aware that confirmation by three witnesses is God's way. The Bible says in 2 Corinthians 13:1, "The facts of the case must be established by the testimony of two or three witnesses." And Matthew 18:16 says, "Everything you say must be confirmed by two or three witnesses." This is how the Lord directs, leads, and helps us put the pieces together.

I had asked God to give me a revelation and help me understand what had happened to Mom. I could see where He was directing me, but what did Psalm 18 mean? I knew over time I would understand what Psalm 18 revealed about my mom's experience. I know from reading my Bible that God revealed secrets, dreams, and mysteries to both Daniel and Joseph. He revealed hidden things to many of His prophets in the past. Ephesians 3:3 claims He does the same now through His Spirit and Word to His people who have learned to listen and hear. Luke 12 says that the Holy Spirit will teach us all things. A prophetic person simply is someone whom God uses to reveal past or future events. So I knew I would find the answers to the mysteries I was looking for in Psalm 18.

On September 14, 2007, one day after Mom and I had flown back home from Baker City, I was cleaning a rental house, and Harvey was fixing the balcony. The Lord spoke to me as I cleaned and said there would be a book about my mom's experience and the title was to be *Hidden in the Valley*.

I stepped outside for a moment to tell Harvey about it. He later came in and said to me, "Your mom walked through the twenty-third Psalm."

That next day, during a festival at Mt. Hood Village Resort, I was asked to speak about my mom's experience by the pastor of Lynch wood Church of God in Gresham. That's where I began putting together Mom's story and told it to about 150 people. I was excited by the crowd's interest and how the story impacted them. Many people came to me afterward, wanting to know more and thanking me for sharing the story. A few newspaper reporters were there and highlighted the story in the *Gresham Outlook* and *Sandy Post*.

I've been amazed as I've discovered the parallels of my mom's experience to Psalm 18 and 23. In conclusion, her survival is a mystery of God. I believe the Lord orchestrated this whole story to show His love, mercy, and justice to the world. He intervened on our behalf, and He proved His word true as my mother walked through the dark valley of death and lived. He proved His love for her and for us. How else did she survive and defeat her enemies, fear, worry, and death?

So we, the family of Doris Anderson, stand up and say, "Who is like the Lord? No one! We will lift Him an anthem of praise."

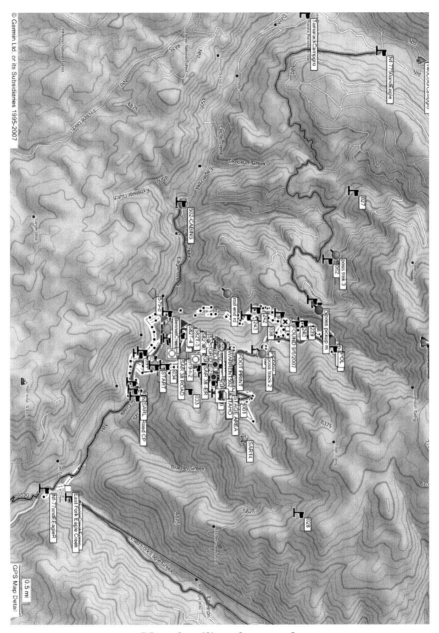

Map detailing the search
"Materials reproduced with the permission of Garmin.
Copyright 2013 Garmin Ltd or it's subsidiaries. All rights reserved."
Search created by Baker County SAR Cordinator Chris Galiszewski

COMFORTER
by Steve De Jesus Olivares

Conclusion
PSALM 18

¹ I love you, LORD;
    you are my strength.
² The LORD is my rock, my fortress, and my savior;
    my God is my rock, in whom I find protection.
He is my shield, the power that saves me,
    and my place of safety.
³ I called on the LORD, who is worthy of praise,
    and he saved me from my enemies.
⁴ The ropes of death entangled me;
    floods of destruction swept over me.
⁵ The grave wrapped its ropes around me;
    death laid a trap in my path.
⁶But in my distress I cried out to the LORD;
    yes, I prayed to my God for help.
He heard me from his sanctuary;
    my cry to him reached his ears.
⁷ Then the earth quaked and trembled.
    The foundations of the mountains shook;
    they quaked because of his anger.
⁸ Smoke poured from his nostrils;
    fierce flames leaped from his mouth.
    Glowing coals blazed forth from him.
⁹ He opened the heavens and came down;
    dark storm clouds were beneath his feet.

¹⁰ Mounted on a mighty angelic being, he flew,
   soaring on the wings of the wind.
¹¹ He shrouded himself in darkness,
   veiling his approach with dark rain clouds.
¹² Thick clouds shielded the brightness around him
   and rained down hail and burning coals.
¹³ The LORD thundered from heaven;
   the voice of the Most High resounded
   amid the hail and burning coals.
¹⁴ He shot his arrows and scattered his enemies;
   his lightning flashed, and they were greatly confused.
¹⁵ Then at your command, O LORD,
   at the blast of your breath,
   the bottom of the sea could be seen,
   and the foundations of the earth were laid bare.
¹⁶ He reached down from heaven and rescued me;
   he drew me out of deep waters.
¹⁷ He rescued me from my powerful enemies,
   from those who hated me and were too strong for me.
¹⁸ They attacked me at a moment when I was in distress,
   but the LORD supported me.
¹⁹ He led me to a place of safety;
   he rescued me because he delights in me.
²⁰ The LORD rewarded me for doing right;
   he restored me because of my innocence.
²¹ For I have kept the ways of the LORD;
   I have not turned from my God to follow evil.
²² I have followed all his regulations;
   I have never abandoned his decrees.
²³ I am blameless before God;
   I have kept myself from sin.
²⁴ The LORD rewarded me for doing right.
   He has seen my innocence.
²⁵ To the faithful you show yourself faithful;
   to those with integrity you show integrity.
²⁶ To the pure you show yourself pure,
   but to the wicked you show yourself hostile.

²⁷ You rescue the humble,
but you humiliate the proud.
²⁸ You light a lamp for me.
The LORD, my God, lights up my darkness.
²⁹ In your strength I can crush an army;
with my God I can scale any wall.
³⁰ God's way is perfect.
All the LORD's promises prove true.
He is a shield for all who look to him for protection.
³¹ For who is God except the LORD?
Who but our God is a solid rock?
³² God arms me with strength,
and he makes my way perfect.
³³ He makes me as surefooted as a deer,
enabling me to stand on mountain heights.
³⁴ He trains my hands for battle;
he strengthens my arm to draw a bronze bow.
³⁵ You have given me your shield of victory.
Your right hand supports me;
your help has made me great.
³⁶ You have made a wide path for my feet
to keep them from slipping.
³⁷ I chased my enemies and caught them;
I did not stop until they were conquered.
³⁸ I struck them down so they could not get up;
they fell beneath my feet.
³⁹ You have armed me with strength for the battle;
you have subdued my enemies under my feet.
⁴⁰ You placed my foot on their necks.
I have destroyed all who hated me.
⁴¹ They called for help, but no one came to their rescue.
They even cried to the LORD, but he refused to answer.
⁴² I ground them as fine as dust in the wind.
I swept them into the gutter like dirt.
⁴³ You gave me victory over my accusers.
You appointed me ruler over nations;
people I don't even know now serve me.

⁴⁴ As soon as they hear of me, they submit;
    foreign nations cringe before me.
⁴⁵ They all lose their courage
    and come trembling from their strongholds.
⁴⁶ The LORD lives! Praise to my Rock!
    May the God of my salvation be exalted!
⁴⁷ He is the God who pays back those who harm me;
    he subdues the nations under me
        ⁴⁸ and rescues me from my enemies.
You hold me safe beyond the reach of my enemies;
    you save me from violent opponents.
⁴⁹ For this, O LORD, I will praise you among the nations;
    I will sing praises to your name.
⁵⁰ You give great victories to your king;
    you show unfailing love to your anointed,
    to David and all his descendants forever.

CUDDLING WITH COWS
by Steve De Jesus Olivares

AFRAID
by Steve De Jesus Olivares

MYSTERIES REVEALED BY PSALM 18

Verse 1: My family loves the Lord because He first loved us.

Verse 2: We asked the Lord to keep Mom safe. We asked the Lord to protect Mom from wild animals. We asked our Savior to rescue her. Jenny, Harvey's sister-in-law, asked the Lord to send animals to keep Mom warm. Mom does remember that Cows let her cuddle up to them and kept her warm.

Verse 3: We asked the Lord, who is worthy of praise, that His name be honored throughout the whole world for rescuing Mom and that He would get the glory for it, and her story became international news.

I had a vision of my mom when she had seen the mother bear and cubs in the moonlight. After seeing them, she had quietly turned around and went back downstream. In the vision, I saw her sitting in the black night with her back up against a tree, scared to death. She pressed against the tree to make sure nothing could sneak up behind her. The Lord said to me, "She was scared out of her mind, but I was always with her and wouldn't let the animals hurt her."

She didn't walk out of the valley because she was afraid. She was not going near the mother bear again.

Verse 4: I believe fear and worry drove Mom out of her mind, and she was truly lost in the woods. She was deceived by fear and worry into believing that she saw officers shoot her husband. She hid from the rescuers trying to save her, fearing that they meant to harm her.

Verse 5: Death joined fear and worry, and they laid a trap to kill Mom in the wilderness. She was naked and dying, and yellow jackets were eating her flesh.

Verse 9: On September 10, Mom told me in the hospital after her deliverance, "I cried out to the Lord and asked Him to help me and, you know, He did; He just woke me up this morning."

Verses 10–19: The Lord was with Mom in the darkness. I can picture Him flying to her side to protect her from her enemies. He blew on Travis and Chris, changing their course so they could save her.

He led the rescuers and used them as His hands. They reached down and drew her out of the deep valley. She was rescued from the powerful demons that hated her and were too strong for her to break free from on her own. They attacked her when she was in distress, but the Lord was her life support.

She was taken to the hospital, a place of safety, where she was restored physically. During her deliverance, the Lord scattered and confused fear, worry, and death. The Lord Jesus Christ opened her prison door and set her free from her captivity. He restored her mind and emotions from the bondage of what oppressed her.

Verses 20–26: Mom was rewarded for the clean and pure life she has lived. She was a virgin when she married. I have never seen her act immorally.

Verse 27: The humble are rescued, and my mother is the essence of humility. Even though she had nothing to eat for two weeks, she was still concerned about the men who had found her and whether they were taken care of before she worried about her own needs.

Verse 28: Mom survived in the darkness without a lantern, flashlight, or even a match, but she did have the Lord, the Light of the World.

Verse 29: We don't fight against flesh and blood but evil rulers of the unseen world, against mighty powers in the dark world. The dark army was denied its victory. The cavalry arrived and carried Mom up the steep canyon wall.

Verse 30: There is no doubt that the Lord proved to my family that His promises are true. My mother is the one who taught me to believe. He was truly a shield of protection for Mom. Who but the Lord did Mom have in that valley?

Verse 31: When it really mattered and Mom had nothing and was unable to save he own life, the Lord, her solid rock, was with her and He was enough.

Verses 32–33: Mom's toes were black from frostbite, yet she didn't lose a single toe. Although she had to go through physical therapy to walk again, she did regain her strength. She still exercises and is strong and active.

Verses 34–48: I happened to be trained for battle, equipped with His strength and knowledgeable in casting out demons and present when they manifested. I asked God to rescue my mom from fear and worry for many years, and I was blessed to be the one at the right place at the right time to help her experience deliverance and walk into freedom. The name of Jesus is mighty and demolishes strongholds. His name subdues enemies and brings victory and safety. We hope this story will help those who are held in strongholds of wrong thinking to break free.

Verses 49–50: We will praise the Lord before the nations. He has given us a great victory. Doris Anderson is now free from fear and worry. Death was denied his victory in the wilderness and forever because she has the promise of eternal life.

PSALM 23

The LORD is my shepherd;
    I have all that I need.
He lets me rest in green meadows;
    He leads me beside peaceful streams.
He renews my strength.
He guides me along right paths,
    bringing honor to His name.
Even when I walk
    through the dark valleys of death,
I will not be afraid,
    for you are close beside me.
Your rod and your staff
    protect and comfort me.
You prepare a feast for me
    in the presence of my enemies.
You honor me by anointing my head with oil.
    My cup overflows with blessings.
Surely your goodness and unfailing love will pursue me
    all the days of my life,
    and I will live in the house of the LORD forever.

MOM'S WALK THROUGH PSALM 23

"The Lord is my shepherd; I have all that I need": We prayed for Mom and Dad before they even left home and put them in the hands of the Good Shepherd. I believe the Lord went ahead of them and was ready to protect them from all the dangers of the wilderness. Jesus demonstrated very clearly through my mom's experience that He can care for His sheep under all circumstances. She did not lack the expert care of her Master; her shepherd was with her.

"He lets me rest in green meadows": After the steep climb from where their Chevy Tahoe was stranded, Mom and Dad took a nap in a green meadow. We also called Bennet Creek Drainage where she went down to the stream and where she was found the parting meadow because that was where my dad last saw her.

I did some studying on the subject of the shepherd and his sheep and found out some interesting facts from Phillip Keller's book *A Shepherd Looks at Psalm 23*. Sheep will not lie down and rest if plagued by fear, friction with the flock, hunger, thirst, or insects. Sheep are very timid and fearful. Anything can startle them and send them running for their lives.

There's a special relationship between a good shepherd and his sheep. A good shepherd loves and takes care of his flock and lays his life down for them. Jesus identified Himself as the Good Shepherd. The shepherd's presence in the field will allow sheep to be able to lie down and rest like nothing else will.

Mom was plagued by fear and worry of both the known and unknown. She was probably agitated and experiencing some friction with Dad because she was hot and thirsty and wanted to go back to the truck.

The wilderness is full of bugs, flies, mosquitoes, and bees. The officers that found Mom covered her with their shirts to keep off the yellow jackets that were eating her flesh.

There's no doubt she was hungry. Mom told Travis and Chris that she had seen officers shoot her husband and that she had seen him fall off his ATV. When Chris asked if she had heard anyone calling her name, she replied, "Oh yes, but I thought it was the ones who shot my husband." She was afraid and running from the ones trying to help her, but her shepherd was with her.

Cheryl, Harvey, and I were put at ease because we all received the same message that Mom was with the Lord within the same hour. We only knew one thing, and that made all the difference: Mom was with the Lord whether she was alive on the mountain or taken to her heavenly home through death. Her shepherd was with her. We could rest in that knowledge. The shepherd was also with us.

"He leads me beside peaceful streams": Mom was thirsty and was led to the stream where she could hear the water. Travis and Chris wanted to look by the water because the nature of an animal when it is not well is to go to water. They were right: they found her lying next to the stream. She was dehydrated when she was found. The doctors were amazed that Mom didn't have parasites from drinking unclean water. Her shepherd was with her. The stream He led her to was pure water.

"He restores my soul": I believe Mom's soul was "cast down." Dad says he watched Mom walk down the road and continued to watch until she was out of sight.

What was Mom's state of mind as she walked away? Dad says she was fine. I don't think so for three reasons. First, she had told Dad she didn't believe that God loved her anymore because her prayers weren't being answered. She thought He was too busy helping other people to help her. Second, she had told her best friend, Mary, that she didn't think she was coming back from the hunting trip. Third, she gave a bag of her precious things she always kept with her to my dad when they parted and asked him to keep them. I believe she was extremely discouraged, feeling uncared for and ready to give up.

"He guides me along right paths, bringing honor to his name": Sheep favor certain spots. They will stay in the same area and pollute the ground until it's diseased and they become thin and sickly if not moved to fresh pasture.

Like a sheep, Travis and Chris said they believed Mom had stayed in the same area the whole fourteen days. The area of ground was worn and revealed evidence of where her favorite spot had been.

She was thin, dehydrated, and sickly when she was found. We had asked God to send the rescuers to find Mom and that she would be restored. We asked for a great testimony to come out of this. We asked that the world would know that God had saved her. We declared that she would live and not die, and that His glory would be revealed on the earth.

"Even when I walk through the dark valleys of death, I will not be afraid, for you are close beside me": Keller said the shepherd leads his flock through the high country in the summer because that's where the best pasture is. It's also the well-watered route.

The shepherd always goes before his sheep and prepares the way for them to ensure their safety. He knows all the dangers of the wild. There are predators such as bears, cougars, and coyotes. Also, there can be sudden storms, mudslides, and avalanches.

Sheep are thin skinned and chill easily. The shepherd knows the mountains are dangerous for his sheep, but he's there to protect them. He knows all about his sheep, always keeping his eye on them. The sheep are content because the shepherd is with them.

Another fact about sheep is that they get cast down, meaning on their back with legs in the air, unable to get on their feet. They will die if not found quickly. Predators, including buzzards, watch for downed animals. They are easy prey.

When Travis and Chris went out looking to recover Mom's body, they were looking for scavenger birds. They heard ravens crying and were alerted and watched for them to indicate where Mom's body was lying. They never did find the birds but knew they were near my mom. When they found her, she was lying on the ground naked, unable to get up on her feet. She would have soon died if not found.

I was with Mom in the hospital when her nurse was washing her hair, and she told me Mom's hair was full of mud, perhaps from a mudslide. There had been two storms in the Wallowas when Mom was out there. The elderly are also thin skinned. How could Mom have survived all this except for the Good Shepherd? He was with her.

"Your rod and your staff protect and comfort me": The shepherd's rod was a sign of his authority and protection. The staff comforted the sheep and got them out of places they stumbled into or became stuck in.

The Lord sent Travis and Chris to find His missing sheep. Besides the shepherd being with Mom, He used these men as His rod and staff to protect and comfort Mom.

The rod and staff were also used to carefully and intimately examine the sheep to make sure everything was well. At this point of the story, Mom was carefully, tenderly, intimately, and skillfully examined by the medical technician, ambulance crew, and hospital staff.

"You prepare a feast for me in the presence of my enemies. My cup overflows with blessings": Keller explained that the high alpine meadows where the shepherd leads his sheep to feed are called tablelands. This table was what King David was referring to when he wrote Psalm 23.

After Mom was brought out of the woods, food baskets, flowers, cards, get-well wishes, and prayers came from all over the world. Many people were drawn into the great celebration with our family because Mom had been rescued and was alive.

Her story became international news. Her picture was on the front page of every newspaper from her little town of Sandy, Oregon, all the way to Edinburgh, Scotland, and London. Chat rooms were debating how she survived. Believers as well as nonbelievers were calling it a miracle.

"You honor me by anointing my head with oil": The mountains swarm with all sorts of winged and crawling insects. Insects torment sheep. The antidote is covering them with an oil mixture. Once the oil is applied, the tormented animal can rest, Keller explained. When going into the valley to research for this book, Travis told me to "get ready for the buggies."

Mom was covered with sores on her arms and legs, which became infected and swollen and began oozing. This was probably caused by insects.

King David's head was anointed with oil by the prophet Samuel as Saul was before him. Anointing the head transferred to a man all that God wanted him to accomplish. The name Jesus Christ means "the anointed one."

With anointing comes power to transform. I saw with my own eyes in the hospital the evidence, once I applied the anointing of the Spirit of God to my mom's mind and submerged her in it the whole day until she was soaked, how her tormentors left her. There was an incredible transformation by the next morning. The demons left. There was night and day difference.

"Surely goodness and mercy will follow me all of the days of my life": There's suffering in life. We can't get around that. But the Good Shepherd is good all the time.

Mom would have perished, but her shepherd was with her. The mountains were cold, and Mom had no heavy coat or blanket, only a light jacket. But her shepherd was with her. By His mercy, she does not remember the suffering.

We, as a family, became better through the suffering. We hope lives will be changed because of our suffering. We will brag on the Lord because He always brings us through, and we can count on His goodness and mercy to be available each morning. He will be there all the days of our lives.

"And I will live in the house of the Lord forever": What could be sweeter than this?

AFTERWORD

Today Mom and Dad live with Cheryl's family. For a time, I also lived with them. My family pooled our resources and helped take care of each other because that's what families do. My sister Cheryl and I continue to work together to make sure our parents remain active and someone keeps an eye on them twenty-four hours a day to ensure their safety. We will continue advocating for our parents and helping each other to make the rest of their lives the best they can be.

After Mom's rescue, she had some short-term memory loss as a result of the hypothermia she suffered. Dad was diagnosed with Parkinson's disease and early dementia five years later. My family learned that Dad had experienced many small strokes and also was suffering from apathy, or brain shrinkage. He more than likely had a stroke at the time of the accident, which would account for his judgment issues, confusion, and strange behavior at the time.

For these reasons, Cheryl was looking for a way to help Mom and Dad with their memory issues. She ultimately found Advocare, a nutrition company founded in 1993. Advocare is a fast-performing vehicle for both health and finances. I found this out when I lost 24.5 pounds in twenty-four days and felt great: no tiredness or food cravings.

Based on personal experience and research, Cheryl, Harvey, and I believe Advocare products are the best nutrition products available. All three of us joined the Advocare team, and now make it our business to help as many others as we can discover and experience the transformation of their health and finances.

Advocare represents freedom and has been an answer to prayers and a solution for my whole family. We give our parents the best body fuel and brain food possible each day. We also get the joy of cooking good meals for them! Mom has no pain in her body, she no longer is a recluse, and she enjoys time with her family and friends. My mother even flew alone to Mississippi to visit her roots; that wouldn't have happened before her accident. She almost got lost at the airport, though, but her shepherd was still looking after her. And she got safely home.

Mom and Dad's trips to the wilderness have ended, except now my dad "time-travels" through his dreams, where his hunting trips are never-ending.

I give thanks for everyone who spent time searching for my mother. I give thanks for all who contributed to her rescue. I give thanks for everyone who cared for my mom and dad and helped them recover from this experience. I give thanks for all the media who told our story and spread the news throughout the world. I give thanks for everyone who cared, prayed, gave of themselves and their resources, and helped my family. Once my mom was lost, but now she is found. She is alive, well, and free. I give thanks for Jesus!

The family

APPENDIX

TIPS FOR PEOPLE WHEN THEY ARE LOST

Search and rescue coordinator Chris Galiszewski provided this information to share:

1. Stay with your vehicle because it can provide shelter, food, and/or water. Also, it's easier to find a car or truck than a single person. Make a camp at the vehicle and build a fire, if conditions permit.
2. Stay on the road. Hunters, hikers, and other people do travel the roads looking for game or exploring the wilderness, and most will stop and help you.
3. Stay together. It's easier to find two people than one person alone.
4. Don't hide from search and rescue teams.
5. Tell someone where you are going and check in with that person. If your plans change, update that person. Have prearranged safeguards, such as calling for help if you don't check it by a specific time or date.

Here are some facts from the James Kim search from November 2006, with more information available on Wikipedia, and the review by the Oregon State Sheriff's Association, which sets the standards for Oregon search and rescue teams:

Oregon Revised Statutes offer specific guidance on how search and rescue operations are to be organized. The Oregon State Sheriff's Association (OSSA) has taken an active role in search and rescue operations at the state level. The OSSA has adopted minimum search and rescue requirements as well as established an advisory council that is responsible to establish minimum training.

As of 2006, 5,889 people were found or recovered by search efforts in Oregon. One hundred twenty-three people have been the subject of search and rescue missions and still remain missing in the state of Oregon. Over the last nine years, 93.7 percent of search missions in Oregon have lasted fewer than twenty-four hours.

This search for my mother and others searches since the James Kim event have set new levels of search theory guidelines for the recovery and rescue of lost or missing persons.

Out of deep gratitude for the Search and Rescue agencies who searched for my mother, a portion of the annual sales from this book will be gifted to them.

RESOURCES

Hiddeninthevalleybook.com
Hiddeninthevalleyfilm.com
Barbarajmoore.com
http://www.motiveeight.me/Barbarajmoore35?refuid=225004260
&refmid=2236#.UVKEC_9WELc.email

BIBLIOGRAPHY

Keller, Phillip W. *A Shepherd Looks at Psalm 23.*

ABOUT THE AUTHOR

My name is Barbara Jean Moore. I am a single mother of two girls, Jordan Ashley, twenty-three, and McKenna Rose, twelve. I was born and raised in the Pacific Northwest and currently live in Washington.

I have known that I was a writer since 1993. I was trying to figure out what my purpose was at that time when a still, small voice inside of me confirmed that I was created to be an author. I had always enjoyed writing and journaling.

In 2004, I began writing *The Journey Home* and am still waiting on the ending of that story. *Hidden in the Valley* is a Pacific Northwest story. The setting is Oregon's Eagle Cap Wilderness, part of the Wallowa-Whitman National Forest. The story discusses this international headlining news after my then-seventy-six-year-old mother was rescued after fourteen days lost in the Wallowa Mountains.

Although I believe I am a good writer, it helped that I had such an amazing story to write. I'm confident that I was the best person to tell this story because of my relationship with my mother and because it's about my family's experience walking through the valley of the shadow of death.

I have always loved communication, both written and verbal, and enjoy starting conversations with others. I love connecting with people and want to make a difference in our world.

I have taken writing classes and workshops, which have helped me sharpen my skills. I love to learn and will continue to seek out opportunities to improve my writing.

I am also an entrepreneur. I have been self-employed more often than not and built a business serving the villages of Mount Hood but chose to close that door to pursue my dream. I am currently building a business that helps people in the areas of health and finances. I hope to add value to their lives and develop mutually beneficial relationships.

I really just want to connect with people and help better their lives if I can. I also hope to write more books.

CONTACT BARBARA

If you would like to have Barbara as a guest at your event or to speak to your audience, please visit her speaking page at:

barbarajmoore.com/speaking

You can also connect with Barbara here:
barb@barbarajmoore.com

Blog: barbarajmoore.com
Twitter: twitter.com/barbjmoore
Facebook: facebook.com/barbarajmooreauthorspage

I welcome your feedback about your experience with *Hidden in the valley* at my website:

Hiddeninthevalleybook.com

Tell me how you feel about *Hidden in the Valley* and read what others are saying.

Discuss Hidden in the valley on FaceBook: facebook.com/ Book named Hidden in the Valley

Communicate with the Author. FaceBook: facebook.com/ Barbarajmooreauthorspage

Read Barbara's blog.

Purchase additional copies of *Hidden in the Valley*.

CPSIA information can be obtained at www.ICGtesting.com
Printed in the USA
BVOW04*1906310314

349319BV00001B/1/P